SPACE ACADEMY

Holiday club programme

for 5- to 11- year olds

© Scripture Union 2012
First published 2012
ISBN 978 1 84427 707 0

Scripture Union
207–209 Queensway, Bletchley, Milton Keynes, MK2 2EB
Email: info@scriptureunion.org.uk
Website: www.scriptureunion.org.uk

All rights reserved. No part of this publication may be reproduced, stored in a retrieval system, or transmitted in any form or by any means, electronic, mechanical, photocopying, recording or otherwise, without the prior permission of Scripture Union.

Scripture quotations are from the Contemporary English Version published by HarperCollinsPublishers © 1991, 1992, 1995 American Bible Society.

British Library Cataloguing-in-Publication Data
A catalogue record of this book is available from the British Library.

Printed and bound in Singapore by Tien Wah Press.

Cover and internal design: kwgraphicdesign
Cover and internal illustrations: Sean Parkes

Main contributors: Steve Hutchinson and Helen Franklin
Additional material by Maggie Barfield, Alison Dayer, Carolyn Edwards, Marjory Francis, Helen Jones, Alice Langtree, Gill Marchant and Alex Taylor

Scripture Union is an international Christian charity working with churches in more than 130 countries.

Thank you for purchasing this book. Any profits from this book support SU in England and Wales to bring the good news of Jesus Christ to children, young people and families and to enable them to meet God through the Bible and prayer.

Find out more about our work and how you can get involved at:
    www.scriptureunion.org.uk (England and Wales)
    www.suscotland.org.uk (Scotland)
    www.suni.co.uk (Northern Ireland)
    www.scriptureunion.org (USA)
    www.su.org.au (Australia)

Contents

Briefing	4
Captain's Log 1: To boldly go …	6
The aims of *Space Academy*	6
Theme and setting	6
Teaching programme	6
Programme breakdown	9
Sample programme	9
Other elements of *Space Academy*	13
Captain's Log 2: Voyage details	14
What are your aims?	14
The children	14
Legal requirements	15
Finances	15
Publicity	15
Planning in detail	15
Setting the scene	17
Captain's Log 3: Lieutenant training	18
Developing people's potential	18
Areas of responsibility	18
Training your team	21
Session 1: The *Space Academy* programme and working with children	21
Session 2: Talking about tough times	24
Session 3: Listening and talking with children	27

Captain's Log 4: Star dates	28
Planning your session	28
Blast off: Taken away	29
Voyage 1: Forbidden food	32
Voyage 2: The difficult dream	39
Voyage 3: Stunning statue	46
Voyage 4: The heavenly hand	53
Voyage 5 In the pit	59
Re-entry: Back to Earth?	65
Captain's Log 5: The engine room	68
Construction/craft	68
Games	70
Tell the story scripts	72
Drama: The final frontier	78
Space Academy theme song	86
Learn and remember song	88
Templates	89
Captain's Log 6: Voyage beyond	92
Follow-up ideas	92

Introduction

Briefing

Space Academy is a seven-day children's holiday club (an opening Sunday service, five club sessions and a closing Sunday service). It has a space theme and explores the early chapters of Daniel. It includes how Daniel and his friends stood up for their faith in a foreign land, despite the opposition, and how God was faithful to them. Children at the club will encounter a God who is wise, powerful, mighty and above all others. But also a God who is interested in helping his people.

This resource book is packed with creative ideas on how to explore these remarkable stories – ideas you can change and adapt to suit your club and context. There are also ideas for construction (craft), games, drama, creative prayer and worship. *Space Academy* has a mixture of up-front presentation and small-group activities, allowing children and leaders to build meaningful relationships with each other and with God.

The holiday club programme is written for the 5 to 11 age group. There are ideas on the *Space Academy* website at **www.scriptureunion.org.uk/ spaceacademy** for extending the age group to include under-5s and/or 11 to 14s. It is for you to decide the best age group for your club and select the activities to fit.

Every effort has been made to ensure this club programme is suitable for children with little or no church background. It is a tool for churches whose desire is to reach out to children and their families outside their church community. It should work equally well for churches wishing to use it as a discipleship resource for children who are already part of the church family.

Space Academy DVD

Children's author and storyteller Bob Hartman will bring the stories of Daniel alive from the exciting exhibitions at the unique National Space Centre, the UK's largest visitor attraction dedicated to space and space exploration. CBBC presenter Gemma Hunt will be on the ground meeting children to ask big questions about God and his amazing universe. Three of the UK's leading 'space scientists', who travel the world teaching others about space, will attempt to answer some of these questions: Professor Russell Stannard OBE, Rev Prof David Wilkinson and Professor Chris Done.

The DVD also contains the *Space Academy* song, backing tracks, training material on listening and talking with children and additional resources.

Daniel's Data

This 48-page booklet contains all the key Bible texts from the Contemporary English Version, along with small-group material, puzzles and extra information.

It is ideal for use with 8 to 11s. *Star sheets* for under-8s are available in this book and can be found at the end of the section for each day (as well as on the DVD and website). There is guidance on how to use both these resources as part of the small-group time in each day's programme, and on page 11. Both *Daniel's Data* and *Star Sheets* help maintain contact with children at home and act as a reminder, in the weeks after the club, of what the children experienced at *Space Academy*. You can buy *Daniel's Data* as multiple copies – see the inside cover for details.

More information on these and other resources can be found on the inside front cover. For all details of the publicity materials produced by CPO, see the inside back cover. (Please note, CPO resources are not available through Scripture Union.)

Space Academy terminology

The Captain
The main presenter of *Space Academy*. They guide children through the session, introducing the different elements and delivering some of the teaching for the day.

The Space Commander
The main storyteller. This person retells the story each day.

Buzz Brain
They relay interesting scientific facts about space and astronauts.

Starbases
The small groups that the children will be part of throughout the club. In these groups, children will explore the Bible, have their refreshments, pray together, play games and do construction.

Astronauts (or Astro-Os)
The children at *Space Academy*.

Lieutenant
Leader of a starbase, helped by an assistant.

The Transporters
The music group.

Super Nova
Leads the phaser-fitness warm-up and maybe the games too.

NB A fuller description of each of these roles can be found on pages 18 and 19.

Visit the Space Academy website
To access downloadable versions of the photocopiable resources and other useful material, go to www.scriptureunion.org.uk/spaceacademy. You can also read about other people's experiences and check out the advice given by other users on the message boards.

CAPTAIN'S LOG 1

Introducing **Space Academy**

To boldly go...

The aims of Space Academy

Space Academy is based on the book of Daniel. Each day the children will see how much Daniel loves God and wants to do the right thing to show this. They will see how God works through Daniel to do amazing miracles, such that the despotic kings of Babylon have to admit that Daniel's God is the greatest.

Space Academy aims to:
- Show how great the supreme God is
- Help the children see what Daniel did to show his love for God
- Invite the children to believe and trust in God as Daniel and his friends did
- Be lots of fun as children share together around the Bible in a friendly and welcoming atmosphere

Theme and setting

Space Academy is all about astronauts, space travel and outer space. You can make it like *Star Wars*, *Star Trek* or *Dr Who*, or any other space setting that your team chooses – you can even make it a mixture. As you set up your venue, think about how you can transform it into a spaceship, mission control centre or even outer space itself! This could be as simple as a painted backdrop (mostly black with white paint spattered on as stars) and various 'planets' or stars hanging from the ceiling.

The space theme is picked up in several different ways:
- The club is introduced and led by the Captain of the spaceship and of the academy where the children are astronaut trainees.
- Every day near the start of the story there is some reference to another planet, which is the cue for flashing lights, space music and everyone lurching from side to side, as when a spaceship is under attack.
- The quiz 'Universe Challenge' has questions about astronauts, stars and planets.
- The children are called astronauts and are led by Lieutenants.
- There are other space-related games and activities.

For more ideas and information on setting up your venue, see page 17.

Teaching programme

The story of Daniel is one of challenge, danger, courage and facing the unknown. Daniel is plunged, against his wishes and as a result of violent conflict, into an amazing adventure where he has to make difficult choices, combat enemies, understand dreams and work miracles, all the time living boldly for God in a world that appears completely alien to him. Though he did not have today's scientific knowledge, it must have felt almost like being on another planet. Each day, in *Space Academy*, the children will discover how much Daniel loves God and wants to live and behave in a way that pleases him. That is not easy or comfortable for Daniel and his friends: while they stand firm for God, others actively oppose them – and have the power to destroy them!

The setting of *Space Academy* picks up echoes of the story of Daniel, with an atmosphere of challenge and adventure in a strange new environment, where everything is different to normal home life. When God's people were taken to Babylon, their world was shattered: everything changed; much was lost;

food, language, the very look, smells and colours around them were strange. As exiles, they were safe in some ways – but not in others. In a light-hearted way, *Space Academy* enables you to parallel their experience (...almost like being on another planet!). Like Daniel, your trainee astronauts will be learning new things about God and trying them out. They will be making amazing discoveries as they voyage to each story and realise how God works through his friends – then and now – and never lets them down. They will be challenged to grapple with what it means to follow God, to live boldly for him – and to have confidence in God's power in the tough times. For Daniel and his friends, this was often a matter of literal life and death. The fictional space setting will enable the children to consider how these young men confronted the reality of their physical risk and spiritual danger, whilst the children themselves are in a secure, positive and supportive environment.

Taking space as a theme may cause some children to ask about life on other planets. You will need to think carefully as a team about how you are going to answer this, bearing in mind that Scripture is silent on the subject.

Daniel – and Jesus?

The *Space Academy* holiday club is based on the book of Daniel, in the Old Testament, but what if we want to talk about Jesus at our holiday club? Where does he fit in? There is not always an obvious springboard from Babylon, around 600 years BC.

It's important that talking about Jesus in your holiday club comes as a natural development of what else is going on and that it is true to the Bible. The daily sessions will point to how you can make genuine links, where appropriate, during the telling of the Bible story itself and during the small group Bible exploration times.

A key time to focus on Jesus is during the 'interview a team member' activity (titled 'On the star spot'). This occurs during your second 'all together' time, if you are following the pattern in this book but could, of course, be at any time during your session. Each day, *Space Academy* gives you advice on how to make these times effective, as the interviewer and interviewee speak from personal experience to explain 'What does this mean to us today?' in the light of Jesus.

Remember, too, that the children will be discovering what it means to be a follower of Jesus simply by being with you! Don't underestimate or undervalue the impact it will have on the children who will experience the reality of your relationship with Jesus day by day.

Scripture Union produces a new holiday club each year so, if you are looking for one based specifically on the life of Jesus, there are several available. Visit **www.scriptureunion.org.uk** and search for 'holiday and midweek clubs' to find out more.

Presenting the Bible story

When you come to the Bible story each day think carefully about how to present it. The *Space Academy* DVD can be used on its own or alongside your method of storytelling. We have provided a script for each day which you can follow word for word for those who need the story set out for them. But if you feel confident, you can adapt the story in a way that you know will relate specifically to your group of children.

If you are going to tell the story yourself, here are three good points to think about every time you tell a story. (There is also an excellent training feature available as a paid-for download on the *Space Academy* website at **www.scriptureunion.org.uk/spaceacademy**.)

1 Work out a really good way of **starting** the story that will grab the attention, so you don't need to tell the children to sit comfortably, or to quieten down. Don't use 'Once upon a time' as this usually indicates a fairy story which is not true. Indeed, some people worry about the term 'story' as that has been used to indicate something that a child has made up, as in 'Are you telling me a story?' If you are worried about this you can get round it by adding, 'and it's all true – it's in the Bible,' or perhaps by having your Bible open at the place and reading something from it as part of your storytelling.

2 Be sure to have **one aim** or major point in telling the story. Any story may have lots of points that you could draw from it, but one main point will focus your storytelling. The main point of each story in this series will probably be the key aim given for the day, but it is worth thinking and praying about it in regard to the children you know are coming.

3 Know how you will **finish** the story. Don't always leave the 'moral' or the meaning of the story till the end. In fact, it is often good to tell a story and not explain it, but leave the children to work it out on their own or in the groups. You could finish with 'I wonder if you have ever thought about…' or with a few moments of quiet to think about what God might want us to know or do from this story, or with a prayer.

SPACE ACADEMY

CAPTAIN'S LOG 1

Voyage schedule

Space Academy covers seven days; five days of holiday club and a Sunday service at the start and the end. If you don't want to run for the full seven days, the *Space Academy* website has a note on how to adapt the material for three or four days.

Sunday service 1: **Taken away**

Key passage Daniel 1:1–7

Key storylines
- The people of Israel are taken from their homes to the very different country of Babylon, where no one knows of, or believes in, God.
- Daniel and his three friends are chosen for special training.

Key aims
- To introduce the Bible story of Daniel and the theme of *Space Academy*.
- To explore the background to Daniel and his friends' move to Babylon, why God allowed this to happen and to consider if God was still with them.
- To intrigue children about what will happen to Daniel and his friends and to invite them to the holiday club to find out.

Day 1: **Forbidden food**

Key passage Daniel 1:8–21

Key storylines
- Daniel, Shadrach, Meshach and Abednego stand firm for God and choose to follow his ways.
- God influences the Babylonian officials to support them and gives the four young men the ability to learn and become wise.

Key aims
- To discover that Daniel and his friends had a choice to make – and that God did not let them down.
- To realise that God helps us when we think about what he wants us to do, and when we do our best to live his way.
- To welcome all the children, start building relationships and have fun together.

Day 2: **The difficult dream**

Key passages Daniel 2:1–6,12–19,31–49

Key storylines
- King Nebuchadnezzar has a dream and is ready to kill all his advisers if they cannot tell him both the dream and its meaning.
- God gives Daniel the secret of the dream, in answer to prayer.
- Daniel tells the king the dream and its interpretation and he, Shadrach, Meshach and Abednego are promoted to high positions in the government of Babylon.

Key aim
- To hear how God gave Daniel the ability to do something that no one else could do and discover why King Nebuchadnezzar declared that God is 'above all other gods and kings'.
- To learn that God helps and protects his friends.
- To continue to build relationships with the children and welcome those who are new to the club today.

Further aim
- To explore the meaning of the king's dream, in the light of what we know about Jesus.

Day 3: **Stunning statue**

Key passage Daniel 3

Key storylines
- Shadrach, Meshach and Abednego risk their lives by refusing to bow and worship a statue.
- King Nebuchadnezzar threatens them with being burned in a flaming furnace but they still refuse.
- They are thrown into the fire but are not harmed – and a fourth person is seen in the fire with them.
- They come out of the furnace and the king acknowledges the power of God and promotes them, again.

Key aims
- To show that Shadrach, Meshach and Abednego stood firm for what they believed and God honoured their faith.
- To demonstrate God's awesome power and discover that worshipping God is the most important thing in the world.
- To continue to build relationships with the children and welcome those who are new to the club today.

Further aim
- To explore the meaning of the story further, in the light of what we know about Jesus.

Day 4: **The heavenly hand**

Key passage Daniel 5

Key storylines
- King Belshazzar mocks God by using treasures from the Temple for his own banquet.
- A hand appears and writes a message on the wall: the king is terrified and no one at the banquet knows what the words mean.

- Daniel explains the message – and it comes true that night when the country is taken over by another powerful nation and Darius becomes king.

Key aims
- To hear how Belshazzar found out that God is real and powerful and how it matters how people treat him.
- To be challenged about our own attitudes to, and relationship with, God.
- To continue to build relationships with the children and be ready to discuss things with them that arise from the stories and activities in *Space Academy*.

Day 5: **In the pit**

Key passage Daniel 6

Key storylines
- Daniel's enemies persuade King Darius to make a law that says people must only pray to him for the next 30 days.
- Daniel prays to God, as he always does, and his enemies tell the king.
- The king has no choice but to obey his own law and has Daniel put into a pit of lions. God keeps him safe.
- In the morning, Darius is relieved and has Daniel brought out of the pit; he calls on everyone to worship God.

Key aims
- To find out what happened when Daniel risked his life by praying to God – and how God answered his prayers and the prayers of the king.
- To realise that God answered Daniel's faithful prayers and the prayer of the non-believing king and to work out what that means for us today.
- To experience a dramatic final day of the holiday club programme together and to encourage the children to return for your closing Sunday service and other future events (depending on what you are planning).

Sunday service 2: **Back to Earth?**

Key passage Daniel 1–6 (as a round-up of the whole adventure)

Key storylines
- God is with his people, wherever they are.
- Daniel and his friends stood firm for God and lived God's way, no matter what the circumstances: we can learn from their example of boldness and quiet courage.
- God did not let them down: we can learn from their example of faith and trust.

Key aim
- To remind all the children of what they have learnt in the holiday club and to share those things with their parents and the wider church family.

Programme breakdown

Each day's programme contains the following elements:

Lieutenants' briefing

Any holiday club's success is built on prayer. This material provides notes to encourage the team to think and reflect personally on each day's Bible story from Daniel. Before the children arrive, spend some time digging into the Bible story. Pray for each other and pray for the children in your club.

During this time, you'll also need to check that you have everything you need for the session (the

Sample programme

This programme runs for 2 hours 30 minutes, not including preparation and clear-up time.

Activity	Running time	Includes
Lieutenants' briefing	30 minutes	Spiritual and practical preparation for the team
Report to Starbase (Small groups)	10 minutes	Introductory activities in Starbases
Action stations (All together)	45 minutes	Up-front Bible teaching, DVD, warm-up, songs, games
Lunar landing	55 minutes	Bible discovery, refreshments, construction, games
Red alert!	30 minutes	Teaching recap, interview, songs, drama, Learn and remember verse
Touchdown	10 minutes	Creative prayer, conversation
Voyage clear-up	30 minutes	Team tidy, debrief and preparation for next session

equipment checklist for each day is a useful way of doing this), make health and safety checks and ensure everything is ready for the children's arrival.

Arriving at Space Academy

The first moments at *Space Academy* are so important! Be welcoming, but not overwhelming, in putting the children and accompanying adults at their ease. Strike a balance between helping parents to see that their children will be safe with you and giving children a sense of the fun that they'll have during the session. Make sure you have enough people at the registration desk (especially on the first day) to show children and their parents to the right groups. It's always helpful to have someone available to answer questions as the parents leave, or to remind them of the collection time, or just to say a cheerful, 'See you later!'

Registration

Make sure that the registration desk is well organised with spare forms and pens for any parents who want to register their children at the door. Have a floor plan of your venue to show where each team is sited, so that parents can find their way round. If possible, have a large plan available a little distance away from the desk so that parents dropping children at more than one group can go back to check the layout without clogging up the registration area.

Report to Starbase

This time is not just a fill-in until the last child arrives. During this time the key aims will be relationship-building and feedback. It is a great time to check out who can remember the Learn and remember verse or the story from previous days. Each day there is an introductory activity to do together. These build on the space theme and allow you plenty of time to chat and get to know each other better in your Starbases. Any astronaut with jokes or pictures for the 'space capsule' should deliver them as they arrive.

Action stations

This section of the programme is designed to be fast-moving and fun. The children are all together for Stadium 1, which is led from the front. It contains the main teaching for the day, together with the other elements outlined below.

Phaser-fitness

This is a fun workout, designed to get the children moving and using up some energy, led by Super Nova. Use any fast sci-fi or space-related music and keep the exercises simple. Be aware of any children with special needs and include some actions that they can do. This section works best when it has been well prepared.

Brain boosters

Buzz Brain introduces two amazing space-related facts related to each day's themes that they will later refer to in the quiz. They will encourage the children to remember the facts to help them with the quiz.

Full throttle

This is an individual challenge led from the front, mainly for leaders to take part in but sometimes for the children. Fast-paced and often messy, it's guaranteed to get people hot under the collar! Encourage the children watching to volunteer their leader and to cheer on all volunteers. Each day's challenge is different and will need a person from the team to make sure all the resources are ready to use at the right moment.

Star songs

Think about the children that you are running this club for. If not many are church children choose songs that don't require them to sing that they believe in God; use songs that tell about how great God is.

There are two *Space Academy* theme songs this year. The main one is about the life of Daniel: you can find sheet music and words for this on page 86. The other is a more general one about space and can be found on the *Space Academy* website **www.scriptureunion.org.uk/spaceacademy**. Whichever you choose to use, these theme songs provide a soundtrack to your club, help develop an identity to your club and are fun to sing! There is also a song to help children learn the Learn and remember verse and the sheet music and words for this are on page 88. There are audio versions for all three songs on the *Space Academy* DVD.

Here are some other suggestions of songs that would work well with the theme:
- So amazing God (starts: He is the world-creating) From *Light for Everyone* CD, SU;
- Twisting back in time From *Light for Everyone* CD, SU
- I try to do what's good From *Reach up* CD, SU

These can be downloaded as individual tracks (for 0.79p each) by going to **www.scriptureunion.org.uk/shop** and typing the song title into the search box.

One giant leap
Each day the Captain will present an activity from the front that involves volunteers, sometimes one child from each group. They will be given different tasks to do on each day, but the task will relate to the theme of the Bible story for that day.

Tell the story
This is the main storytelling section of the club. The Space Commander tells the day's story using various props or visual aids. The children are encouraged to take part in different ways each day.

The *Space Academy* DVD contains five storytelling episodes, written and told by Bob Hartman, that help you tell the Bible story. If you don't have any strong storytellers, you may choose the DVD as the primary storytelling tool. Alternatively, you might choose to do the live retelling and reinforce it with the DVD. See page 4 for more details about the DVD.

Universe challenge
This is a short quiz to recap the facts of the Bible story, the amazing space facts and some of the events of the day so far. Some suggestions for questions are given for each day, but you'll need to add more of your own questions. There are also suggestions for different methods of scoring which are based on random selection rather than skill, which ensures no particular team comes out top all the time. Keep the style of questions varied (such as asking for a straight answer, providing a choice of two or three answers, or even using pictures for some questions).

Data check
The Captain sums up the story and gives some further explanation and application to the children's lives. Make this punchy and to the point, so that it doesn't go over the children's heads – it should leave the children thinking and challenged!

Prayer
To conclude Action stations you may want to pause here to give children an opportunity to think about what they've learnt and to pray silently.

Lunar landing
The astronauts move into their Starbases for Bible exploration, construction, games and refreshments. You can choose to do the construction and games in Starbases or all together. It depends on what team and facilities you have.

Cafe Cosmos
This is the time when the astronauts have their refreshments. Each day make sure you have refreshments that are suitable for children of other faiths. The easiest way is to make sure they are suitable for vegetarians (eg no gelatine or pork products) and that they contain no nuts. Do tell everyone that the food is OK otherwise they might assume it isn't and not have any.

Use your imagination to come up with refreshments that fit the space theme. A simple and healthy option might be Asteroid Snacks. Slice the bottom off a melon so it sits flat. Skewer fruit pieces with cocktail sticks and insert the ends into the melon. Cover the melon with fruit spikes. Let the astronauts pull the skewers and eat the fruit, being careful not to hurt themselves on the cocktail sticks.

Bible discovery
The Lieutenants help the children to examine the story in the Bible. Our aim is to help them to learn how to read the Bible for themselves and think about how it relates to their lives, by reading the story they have just heard. The *Daniel's Data* booklets (8-11s) or the *Star Sheets* (5-7s) will help the children to work out what the Bible means for them. It is important to make sure that the Lieutenants are well prepared for this time; this is vital if we are to fulfil our aims for the club in helping children to respond to God.

Shuttlecraft
Making a craft or building a construction has two particular purposes: it gives the children something to take home from the club that will act as a reminder; also the time spent making it is a good opportunity for Lieutenants to chat with their teams. You may find that you can have deeper conversations in this time – when everyone is busy looking at their craft – than when you have eye contact in Bible discovery. Therefore, make good use of the time to build friendships and chat about the day's teaching a little more, especially in relation to

the children's lives. See the resource bank on page 68 for construction/craft with a space theme, or for further inspiration see *Ultimate Craft*.

Fit for space
Games used during *Space Academy* can be found on page 70. For further inspiration, see *Ultimate Games*, which contains hundreds of ideas that might be suitable for your club. Make sure you risk-assess these activities and collect all the necessary materials beforehand. 'Fit for space' is also another good opportunity for leaders and children to chat and build relationships.

Red alert!
During this time, the children are all together for activities led from the front.

Space capsule
As the children return from their Starbases, the Captain should read some of the messages and jokes left in the 'space capsule'. The space capsule will be used at Sunday service 1 to give children the idea of what is required. On Voyage 1, the Captain should explain that the capsule is where astronauts can secretly leave their jokes and messages and that, each day, they will read out some of the jokes and show some of their pictures. The space capsule could be made out of a large, upturned popcorn box and a cardboard base added. This could all be covered in silver foil and various buttons and knobs added. It also needs to have a suitably 'space age' door cut out so that children can post their messages in it.

Data recall
The Space Commander recaps the teaching points from the story and what the children have discovered during Lunar landing. Again this should be punchy and to the point. This is not a talk or a teaching time but a recap.

Cosmic code
Each day, the children will be challenged to learn the verse for the week (Proverbs 3:5,6 GNB). A different activity is given each day to help learn the verse, and the Learn and remember verse song is also available (see page 88 and the *Space Academy* DVD). The Learn and remember verse is the same for the whole week, but there are suggested activities using a different verse for each day on the *Space Academy* website, if you want to follow that route.

On the star spot
Each day, a different Lieutenant or Ensign is interviewed. Choose them carefully, as they need to have a story that relates to the day's theme and is suitable to be shared with the children. This interview gives the children the chance to see how the Bible teaching relates to everyday life and what it means to us today in the light of Jesus.

As well as a question that fits the theme, encourage the children to write down any questions they'd like to ask the Lieutenant and to post these in the space capsule. You may want to offer small rewards, eg Mars bar, Milky Way or Starbursts, for the best question of the day.

Drama: The final frontier
The crew of the Starship (insert name of club/town) are given instructions from Mission Command to spread the good news of goodness, kindness, generosity, honesty and mercy around the planets of the Delta Quadrant. On their travels they encounter an alien who turns out to be made of jelly, the planets Ping and Pong and their arch enemy, Odor. He is out to thwart their plans and ultimately to destroy them. On Day 4 he puts them in a life-threatening situation but Mission Command saves the day. The drama is not designed to be a primary teaching tool, but a reinforcement of the theme and a chance for some slapstick fun!

Final orbit
This wraps up the all-together time with the theme song and maybe another song the children have enjoyed. Include a prayer here too, thanking God for your time together.

Touchdown
Each day finishes with a creative prayer activity for the Starbases to do. Alternatively, you could finish off anything from the club that still needs work (pages from *Daniel's Data*, the *Star Sheets* or the construction).

Lieutenants should make a point of saying goodbye to each child and reminding them of the next session.

Voyage clear-up
It may be that some of the team have their own children at *Space Academy* and are unable to stay for long when the programme ends. As a minimum, bring everyone together to check any problems, briefly remind people of tomorrow's activities and pray for the Holy Spirit to be at work in the children.

If you have time and the facilities, the team could share lunch together to round off the day.

Other elements of Space Academy

Services

The programme contains two services, one to start the club and one to finish. These are designed to be an integral part of the club for the children. This is to help you encourage children and their families from outside your church community to come into a church service. Research shows that if you advertise the club as including the services as well as the club days (so a seven-day programme rather than a five-day one), children and families with little or no church background are more likely to attend. However, children who don't attend this first service will still find it easy to join the club on Voyage 1. It is also great to commission the team and get your congregation praying, but this can be done during a service before the first Sunday of *Space Academy*. This means that the first Sunday service of the club has a clear aim (and an earlier commissioning will encourage the church to pray as you prepare, as well as when the club is taking place).

Under-5s resources

For details of resources to use with 5s and under, visit the *Space Academy* website (**www.scriptureunion.org.uk/spaceacademy**). The resources follow the same Bible passages and themes as the main programme.

11 to 14s resources

For details of resources to use with 11 to 14s, visit the *Space Academy* website. The resources follow the same Bible passages and themes as the main programme.

14 to 18s – young leaders

Having young people help out at a holiday club is a fantastic way of discipling and training them in leadership. For training materials for use specifically with 14 to 18s in leadership, go to the *Space Academy* website.

Having a shorter club

If you are planning to run your club over three or four days, rather than five, go to the *Space Academy* website for guidance on how to adapt the material for a shorter club.

Family activities

It is a good idea to include some events in your club for families to attend all together. This will give you a chance to meet and get to know the families of the children who are coming to *Space Academy*. Get your whole church involved in organising food or running activities. Here are a few things you could try:

- **Games**: organise a family games event, using some of the games ideas from pages 70–72. Rocket launch and Gravity pull would be particularly suitable. Families could work together, or you could pair a family from your church community with one new to the church, to help build relationships.
- **Construction**: use some of the construction ideas on pages 68–70 to put together a family session. Activities such as wood turning, pyrography and other more robust crafts are great for encouraging family members to work together (for instance, fathers and sons). You could combine construction and games into one event.
- **Family barbecue**: these events are always popular and can be quite simple to run! Alongside the food, you could run games or construction. Or how about a family quiz? Ask questions about space or the stories from Daniel (for the children).
- **Big-screen events**: There are some amazing videos with images of the universe readily available, but for something with a Christian content, try Louis Giglio's 'Indescribable' available on the internet, where he reignites the sense of wonder at God's amazing creation.

None of these ideas are groundbreaking in themselves but, run in conjunction with the club, they can involve more of the church community in the club, introduce the church to people with little or no previous contact in a relaxed atmosphere and start to build relationships.

CAPTAIN'S LOG 2

Setting up a holiday club

Voyage details

Planning Space Academy
When starting to think about running a holiday club, some big issues need to be tackled.

What are your aims?
The broad aims of *Space Academy* are on page 6, but each individual holiday club will have its own specific aims. *Space Academy* can provide a manageable, creative and fun way of reaching out to the children of your neighbourhood with the good news of Jesus. It can provide an excellent opportunity to blow any misconceptions away and to reveal to them a God who loves them powerfully.

Here are some aims which you might choose for your club:
- To attract new children to join your Sunday groups or other children's activities.
- To develop your leaders' gifts and experience.
- To present the gospel to children who've never heard it.
- To provide an opportunity for children to make an initial or further commitment to follow Jesus.
- To get to know the children in your church.
- To provide a project to encourage your church to work together.
- To establish links with the children's families.
- To encourage cooperation with other churches or groups in your area.
- To launch an ongoing children's group based on the *Space Academy* theme.
- To give parents a few mornings off in the school holidays.

Any or all of these aims may be appropriate, but you'll have to decide what you want *Space Academy* to achieve in your situation. If you have several aims, you'll need to decide which are the most important. You'll also need to evaluate *Space Academy* afterwards, to see if you met your aims. Decide now how you'll do that. How will you measure success? Try the aims form on the *Space Academy* website or DVD and work together to decide on your aims.

The children
Once you have set your aims, you'll be able to make other key decisions such as:

Who will you invite to Space Academy?
- Do your aims relate to the children already involved in your church, or those outside it?
- How many children do you want to involve? If your main aim is to get to know the children better, you might need to restrict numbers. On the other hand, if you want to present the gospel to children who haven't heard it, you may want as many as possible to attend.
- What age range(s) do you want to target with *Space Academy*? Do you want to cater for an age range that is well represented in your groups, or one that isn't? Will you be able to tailor the activities in a way that will appeal to a wide age range? *Space Academy* is designed for use with children between the ages of 5 and 11. See page 13 for information on where to find resources to use with other age groups.

When will you run your club, and for how long?
You'll need to fix the date for your holiday club early enough for people to take it into account when they book their holidays. It is also essential that the dates

do not clash with other holiday clubs in the area, activities already booked at your premises, holidays organised by local schools, holidays/camps for local Boys' Brigade, Girls' Brigade, Cub or Brownie groups. You may also want to avoid clashing with carnivals or local events, although another option is to tie in with these events intentionally and benefit from the buzz around the local area. The summer break is the most obvious time to hold your club but you could consider running it in a half-term holiday or the Easter holidays instead. You could also consider running your club on Sundays through the summer if your other sessions stop running, but this needs careful planning.

The potential leaders' availability will have the most effect on the duration of your holiday club. If most of your leaders need to take time off work, it may not be practical to run a full five-day club.

If you are planning to run your club over three or four days rather than five, go to the *Space Academy* website (**www.scriptureunion.org.uk/spaceacademy**) for guidance on how to adapt the material for a shorter club.

Legal requirements

There are various legal requirements you will need to be familiar with and conform to as you prepare for your holiday club. These include having a child protection policy in place, providing adequate space in your venue, meeting adult to child ratios, insurance. To obtain up-to-date information on all of these requirements, go to the *Space Academy* website.

Finances

You'll need to consider your financial resources. Work out what you'll need money for. Examples might include:
- craft materials
- refreshments
- materials for the scenery
- photocopying/printing costs
- hire of premises
- hire of equipment such as a video projector
- *Space Academy* resource books for your leaders
- resources such as the *Space Academy* DVD and *Daniel's Data*
- prizes or presents for the children

Do you need to do some fund-raising? Or will you charge a small fee for children to attend *Space Academy*? Research shows that in many cases, making a charge for a club has no effect on the number of children who come. Indeed, some parents may value a club they have had to pay for more highly than something that is free.

Publicity

The best way to ensure you have plenty of children at your holiday club is for the event to be well publicised. There is material available from CPO to help you with this. See the inside back cover for details. Here are some things to consider:

Posters and flyers
Use these to advertise *Space Academy*.

Letters and forms
How about sending a letter or invitation card to every child your church has contact with? Or you might distribute letters to all the children in your area, maybe through the local schools. Your letter could enclose an application/registration form to be returned to you. You may also need a follow-up letter which will enclose a consent/medical form, and perhaps a *Space Academy* badge.

School assemblies
You may have a local Christian schools worker, or people from your church who are involved in schools ministry. Or you may have some church members who are teachers. If so, they could promote your *Space Academy* event in a school assembly, if the school is happy for them to do so.

Press releases
Holiday clubs provide the kind of story that local papers love to cover. By getting a story in the press, you'll increase the appeal of your holiday club and show that the church(es) involved are reaching out into your local community. Please mention Scripture Union in your press releases or advertising as positive publicity as, ultimately, this allows us to improve resources like our holiday club material. If you have a good relationship with your local press, then make contact in the usual way and inform them of your event. If this is something you have never considered, a press release template is available on the *Space Academy* website. Include your club's details and send the press release to your local paper.

Prayer cards/bookmarks
It is important to keep your church informed about your event. Prayer cards or prayer bookmarks can help your church members pray for your holiday club – before, during and after your *Space Academy* event.

Planning in detail

In the few months before *Space Academy*, you'll need to consider and organise the following aspects.

Presentation and teaching
How will you adapt the material to suit your particular age group(s)? What audio/visual aids will you need? Will you need amplification or video projection equipment? Who will be the Captain and the Space Commander?

Programme priorities
You may not have time to fit in all the activities that are suggested. Within Starbase times, especially during Lunar landing, you could get so engrossed in general conversation that you never start on the Bible discussions, so be sure to plan carefully.

Imagine filling a jar up to the top with pebbles. You might think it is now full, but try adding some smaller stones and you'll find there is room for them. Is it full now? Try pouring in water, and you will see that only then is the jar really full. But if you put in this amount of either small stones or water first you would not then get everything in! When planning, make sure you put in the essentials first – up-front Bible teaching and discussion time in groups. Then add the less vital but still important things, and finally the parts that 'fill it up'.

Music
Choose the songs for the week, and gather the musicians together to rehearse them. It's good to have a number of musicians playing a variety of instruments, but you'll need to make sure you have enough stage space for other things too! Choose a few new songs and a few old favourites. Make sure you include non-confessional songs, so that the children are not singing words they might not believe. If you don't have musicians in your team, you could use backing tracks or simply sing along to a CD/MP3.

Drama
Do you need to adapt the script to fit the number or gender of your cast members, or the limitations of your venue? How much rehearsal time will you need? How will you obtain or make the necessary props, costumes and scenery?

Training
Undertaking some basic skills and knowledge training is vital for the success of the holiday club. You should aim to have at least two sessions together in preparation, and you should ensure that these are more or less compulsory for team members. As part of these sessions, the vision and practicalities of *Space Academy* can also be outlined. Training is outlined in Captain's Log 3, starting on page 18.

Lunar landing
You'll need to think about how you are going to stage this small-group/craft/games time. What you do depends on your aims and the resources you have available.

- You could have every Starbase doing the same activity on the same day. This means that only one simple explanation from the front is needed, and group leaders can help each other. It also helps to develop relationships within the Starbases. This does, however, require a lot of resources, and activities which suit this format are limited.
- Alternatively, you could set up activities for the whole week and children could rotate around these activities. This means fewer resources are needed for each activity, more activities are possible, and different leaders can take responsibility for leading the same activity each day. However, it is harder to theme each activity to the day's teaching. Some groups will not have their Lieutenant with them during this time if they are leading another activity. You will probably also need specific areas that can be dedicated to each activity, and your venue may not be large enough.

Construction/craft
Where will you get the necessary materials and equipment? Do you need to ask your congregation to collect particular items? A dedicated craft team can be very useful, especially in the run-up to *Space Academy*. This team should collect the necessary materials. They'll also be able to make templates and patterns for the children to draw around or cut out. The craft team should make up prototypes of the craft, and pass on any hints to the Lieutenants.

Involve local schools in amassing reusable material to use during the week (glass jars, plastic bottles, travel magazines for collages, etc). This gets people actively contributing to the club before it has begun, including the children, and alerts the school, to the club, bringing extra publicity.

Games
Consider what games you can play based on the number of children, your venue and the equipment you have. Make sure you have all the equipment you need.

Data protection
How will you maintain the confidentiality of the information you receive on the registration forms? Make sure you abide by the principles of the Data Protection Act. Visit dataprotectionact.org for more information, including the eight principles of protecting data.

Accidents
Make sure you have at least one person who is a trained first-aider with a current first-aid certificate and access to an up-to-date first-aid kit. (This is not a legal requirement but it is important to take reasonable precautions to oversee the welfare of those in your care.) The whole team should know who is responsible for first aid. You will also need an accident book to record any incidents. This is essential in the event of an insurance claim. The matter should be recorded, however small, along with details of the action taken. For other health and safety information visit **www.rospa.com**.

Fire procedures
It is essential that the whole team knows the emergency procedures, including the location of fire exits and assembly points, and where to access a telephone in case of emergency. Ensure you keep all fire exits clear.

Prayer team
Make sure you have a team of people committed to pray throughout the preparation and the club itself. Keep the whole church well informed too. The prayer team should keep on praying for the children in the club in the months after *Space Academy* finishes.

Use of the Bible
One of the aims of *Space Academy* is to help children explore and read the Bible for themselves. So each day during Lunar landing, when you move on to discussing the passage, help the children find it in the Bible or in *Daniel's Data* and learn to look for answers there. Use a translation that is easy for children to read (Good News Bible, Contemporary English Version or International Children's Bible).

Setting the scene
Choosing a venue is a very important issue. Sometimes a community hall or school is a well-equipped, neutral venue that can be non-threatening for children and parents outside the church. However, you may wish to use this opportunity to introduce the children and parents to your church building. This can also help save on the cost of hiring an alternative venue. The venue does need to have enough space for the number of children and the types of activities you are planning. You will need access to the venue before the holiday club to ensure the necessary preparations can be made.

Setting up the room
The holiday club will be greatly enhanced if the main room you are using is transformed into a mission control centre, a spaceship, or even outer space itself! This will help create a wonderful atmosphere and spark the children's imaginations. You will need to think creatively about how you can transform your venue into an exciting place. The imaginative use of cardboard, wood, paint, silver foil and other materials can make a real difference. You could decorate globe-shaped paper lampshades of various sizes to hang from the ceiling as planets, use fluorescent paper for stars and black paper spattered with white paint for the night sky. The following websites are great sources of visual inspiration: **www.nasa.gov**; **http://hubblesite.org**; **www.spacecentre.co.uk**.

The stage area
You will need a focal point at the front from which the Captain can run the programme. Think about where you will do your dramas and where the band will be positioned. You will also need to decide where the projection screen should be located. A draped-off area or an attached room needs to be provided for the actors in the drama to come out of. The boundary for the stage area could be marked by a masking tape line across the floor. You could think about having a lunar landscape on the stage, with a black backdrop and papier mâché hills, craters and moon boulders on the floor.

Starbase locations
The rest of the room can be split up into Starbase locations. The Starbases could be named after planets – ie, Mercury, Venus, Earth, Mars, Jupiter, Saturn, Uranus, Neptune and Pluto. If you have more groups you could also include the names of space shuttles such as Columbia, Discovery, Atlantis, Endeavour, Challenger and Enterprise. If possible, decorate the walls in these areas with black paper and encourage the children to add rockets, satellites, stars, planets and spacemen during 'Report to Starbase'. It may be best to keep chairs out of the way, except for those who cannot sit on the floor, so that the room can be used for the energetic sections of the programme without objects getting in the way.

Fill the screen
If you are using a video projector or OHP, use a default image when it is not being used, so that the screen is never blank. Use something simple, like the *Space Academy* logo or a photo or video of the night sky. The Hubble website **hubblesite.org** has some amazing images to download. The logo and other artwork are available on the DVD-ROM section of the *Space Academy* DVD or on the website.

CAPTAIN'S LOG 3

Working with your team

Lieutenant training

Developing people's potential

As well as being a time of great fun and development for the children attending, a holiday club is also an important time for the adults leading and helping out. Helping with a holiday club can be a big step for people in the development of their gifts and ministries.

How does a holiday club develop people's potential?
- It involves people in the church who don't usually work with children.
- It is an opportunity for people of all ages to work together in a way that may not happen at any other time of the year. (A regular comment at one holiday club from team members is, 'This is the best week of the year in church!' It's probably the most demanding and tiring too!)
- It develops people's gifts and lets them take risks.
- It discovers people's untapped gifts and enthusiasms – eg, you may have amateur astronomers in your congregation.
- It provides a structure for the overall leadership of the club/church to seek out and encourage people to 'have a go'. Don't rely on issuing a general plea for volunteers but look at who you have available and ask people personally, giving them good reasons why you think they could fulfil whatever task you have identified. (This suggests that you believe in them and they are far more likely to agree to get involved!)

Areas of responsibility

A successful holiday club requires a variety of support teams to be set up and individuals to take responsibility for different areas of the programme. Listed below are some of the different teams you will need and some of the key roles people will need to assume before, during and after the event. Some people will be able to play more than one role for *Space Academy*, if you have a small team. For a large team you might want more than one leader to play the Captain.

Core planning team

All the helpers should be involved in planning and preparing for *Space Academy*, but you will need a smaller team to coordinate things and make some initial decisions. As well as the holiday club's overall leader, this should include your most experienced leaders, your minister and your children's workers.

Fleet admiral

This is the overall leader and coordinator, ideally someone who is not involved in the presentation. Their role would be to:
- Make any on-the-spot decisions such as accepting extra children at the door.
- Keep the whole programme to time, moving things on when necessary.
- Look at the quality of presentation, watching out for problems such as too much banter between the teams and the Captain.
- Watch out for children who are not joining in well and helping them to become part of things.
- Be the person to whom everyone would report in the event of a fire.

The Captain

This is the up-front presenter of the club. They should be confident on stage and have experience of leading a programme in a fun but flexible manner. Since they are the person doing the teaching application and reinforcement, they will need to be prepared on what they are going to say.

The Space Commander
This person is the storyteller. As such, they must be a confident and skilled communicator. They need to prepare the story thoroughly and be happy telling it to a group of children. You could use a different person each day, if you don't have one member of the team who could put in this much work. If you are only using the DVD to tell the story, you won't need this role.

Buzz Brain
This is a small role that would be suitable for a junior member of the team. They need to be able to speak clearly and have a good memory for detail. They could play this straight or as an eccentric professor who uses very long words. They could wear flashing crazy hair available from websites such as www.glow.co.uk to show how much their brain 'buzzes'! They could also carry around a file called 'Buzz Brain's Brain Boosters'.

Lieutenants
Each small group needs a leader called a Lieutenant. Each Lieutenant should be at the club every day and will be the person with whom the children have the most personal contact. The Lieutenant's role is to get to know the children so that they feel welcome and comfortable at *Space Academy*. The programme is designed to give the Lieutenants enough time in their Starbases to have meaningful discussions, including ones that apply the teaching programme to the children's lives.

They should coordinate all small-group activities and sit with their Starbases during the up-front times. The Lieutenants should have a copy of the register, be aware of any special needs and ensure that the children all leave safely at the end of the day's session.

Ensigns
The role of the Ensigns is to support the Lieutenants and ideally should also be available every day. This is a good way to develop the leadership skills of young or inexperienced team members.

All team members should be given training in dealing with children, especially in relation to physical contact and not being with children alone out of sight of others, but Lieutenants and Ensigns especially need to be aware of child protection issues and policies.

If you have a large holiday club, you may choose to appoint Lieutenant Commanders to oversee six or eight Starbases who are all in one age range. It is best if these coordinators do not have a group of their own.

Super Nova
This is the fitness instructor who leads a simple aerobic workout each morning to help the children expend some energy at the start of the session. They should keep the actions simple, and remember to include moves suitable for any children in your club who have additional needs. There are suggestions each day for including moves related to the Bible theme for that day.

Drama team
The drama involves 11 characters, although some of the parts could be doubled up. The drama team need to be reasonably confident as actors with the ability to project their voices. The prewritten sketches are somewhat messy and silly and will need some coordination. The team should be willing to learn their lines and to practise each sketch until they can perform it with confidence.

One of the drama team (or another person) needs to take the responsibility of Props Manager, and collect and prepare all the props.

The Transporters [the worship band]
Having a live band can add something special to a holiday club. If you can't use live music, then sing along to a CD. Could The Transporters be creatively dressed? If you don't have a live band, you could have a group of dancers instead. They could lead everyone in some actions to the songs, either with existing actions or their own.

Printing and publicity team
A small team, including at least one computer-literate person, should take responsibility for all the design, printing and publicity for *Space Academy*. Your aim should be to produce publicity that is visually impressive, consistent, accurate and attractive.

The publicity will need to be colourful and use the *Space Academy* logo (available on the DVD or website), an attractive child-friendly font, pictures and clip art. The publicity team could take responsibility for:
- Posters and fliers to advertise *Space Academy*.
- Registration forms for the children to fill in (see sample version on the website).
- Consent forms for parents/guardians/carers (see sample version on the website).
- Invitation cards or letters to go with the appropriate forms.
- Forms for potential team members, including an indication of roles they'd like to take on. You should also send CRB forms out with these forms

to team members who have not already had clearance.
- Notes and training materials for the team. Even if someone else writes this material, the printing and publicity team should be responsible for the layout.
- Name badges for the team members and for any adults who are on site and part of *Space Academy*.
- Signs and notices. These will be needed around the site, including the main hall, entrances, toilets and areas that are out of bounds. These should use the same typeface and colours as other materials to maintain the consistent *Space Academy* scheme.
- Prayer cards/bookmarks – prayer pointers to help church members to pray for the holiday club before, during and after *Space Academy* events.

Registration team

Responsible for:
- Allocation of children to groups.
- Checking children in and out each day.
- Checking forms are completed fully.
- Keeping a check on team sizes if more children register during *Space Academy*.
- Ensuring each child is to be picked up or has permission to walk home by themselves. If you have a lot of children attending the club, it can be hard to keep track of who has permission to collect which child, especially when parents help each other out. A collection slip, which can be given to the adult who will pick the child up, is on the *Space Academy* website.

If you are advertising the club through local schools or community groups, provide children with booking forms in advance which can be filled out and sent back to the leader of the holiday club, school office or community group leader. This allows you to allocate children to groups in advance and will inform you of dietary requirements, medical issues and physical, educational or behavioural special needs. Do remember to check these when planning the club activities! A register can be made, based on the names and ages provided. A copy of the register must also be given to each group leader in case of a fire or emergency.

In some contexts, pre-registering is not practical, therefore ensure on the first day that there are plenty of volunteers available to help greet the children and their parents or carers and to provide them with the registration form to fill in. Children should not attend the event if permission has not been granted. As this can be a lengthy process, you might like to open the doors earlier on Day 1 and, during registration, engage the children in parachute games, up-front games or a short film.

Refreshment team

This team will play a vital role during the week. They will be responsible for:
- Checking with the registration team that you have no children with food allergies.
- Obtaining and preparing the refreshments for the children.
- Tidying up after the refreshments have been given out.

For this team to work efficiently you may like to choose one person to coordinate the group. If you are providing anything more than a drink and a biscuit, you should have someone with a food hygiene certificate. Think about using (recyclable) disposable cups or bottles to save on washing-up time.

Security

The person in charge of security will be responsible for ensuring that no child leaves the building unless they have permission to do so, and that only children or adults who are part of *Space Academy* are allowed to enter the building or area set aside for the club.

It is important for each team member to have an appropriate, clearly labelled badge to identify them and their role. The children registered for *Space Academy* should each have their own badge which should be taken off before they leave the club. Any adult or child on site not wearing an appropriate badge should be challenged.

First-aider

Aim to have at least one member of your team with a valid first-aid certificate. If possible have assistants too – a male for the boys and a female for the girls. These people will need a current first-aid certificate and access to a first-aid kit. You will also need an accident book to record any incidents or accidents. (This is essential in the event of any insurance claim. A record of the matter should be noted, along with details of action taken. It should be countersigned where appropriate.)

Health and safety person

This person will need to plan how you will evacuate the building in the event of a fire. Check that fire escapes are kept clear, that the team members know the position of fire extinguishers and know what the fire alarm – or noise that means 'leave the building immediately' – sounds like. Each Lieutenant should be a roll-call marshal for their teams. The health and safety person is in charge of clearing the building and dealing with the emergency services, but they should allocate responsibility for checking other areas of the building (toilets, snack bar, etc) to other team members who will be present each day. You may want to incorporate a fire drill into your programme early in the week. The children will be used to this from school, but it might help the adults!

They should also make sure all the activities are adequately risk-assessed before the club starts.

Construction [craft] and equipment
Someone should take responsibility for making sure that everything that is needed for the construction (craft), creative prayer and Starbase activities is in the correct place at the right time. Get as much as possible of the craft prepared in advance; there may well be church members who, while they can't help at the club itself, will be happy to help with cutting out, etc.

Try to prepare a finished version of each item to show the children what they are making and provide everything needed for each team's vanity case (pens, paper, modelling clay, etc). Each day one of the craft team should explain how the craft is made and supervise the activity, even if it is done in the Starbases.

Technical manager
The amount of technology used will vary with the size and nature of each club. A technical manager could take responsibility for:
- **Visual** – OHP or laptop and projector, screen, or DVD and TV.
- **Audio** – PA for presenters and band, CD/MP3 player.

Training your team
However experienced your team, there are two key areas to cover in training: good practice in working with children and delivering the *Space Academy* programme itself. Here is a suggested programme for three training sessions. However, this material could easily be spread over several sessions.

Session 1
- **Practicalities**: Basic outline of *Space Academy*, learning the theme song, daily structure, etc
- **Skills**: Leading a small group
- **Skills**: Praying with children
- **Skills**: Reading the Bible with children
- **Prayer**: For *Space Academy* and all who come

Session 2
- **Skills**: How to talk with children about tough times
- **Understanding**: the needs of children facing tough times
- **Skills**: Helping children respond to Jesus
- **Understanding**: Working with special or additional needs
- **Understanding**: Working with children from other faith backgrounds
- **Prayer**: For *Space Academy* and all who come

Session 3
- **Skills**: Listening and talking with children
- Why it matters
- How to do it
- **Practicalities**: Getting the best from the DVD training feature

Session 1
The Space Academy programme and working with children
Use this session to go through some of the practical aspects of the club, to help your team understand what will be expected of them and to begin to consider the children who will come to *Space Academy*.

Welcome
Make sure you give the team a big welcome, ensuring refreshments are freely available, with the *Space Academy* theme song playing in the background as people arrive.

Practicalities
Space Academy
Explain the overall themes of *Space Academy* (see page 6) and how Daniel and his friends stood up for God and trusted him in a foreign land. Give an overview of the different roles that people will have. Introduce the team to the Learn and remember verse (see page 12), the *Space Academy* theme songs, the Captain, the Space Commander, Buzz Brain and the other recurring elements of the programme.

Take the team through a day's programme, making sure that everyone knows where all the different parts will take place and their responsibilities in each one.

The aims of *Space Academy*
Make sure everyone has a copy of the general aims of *Space Academy* (see page 6) and the specific aims for your club. Split into smaller groups to discuss these aims – can the groups identify any other aims?

This will help you refine your aims and encourage your team to take ownership of them.

Legal requirements
Cover health and safety, risk assessments, fire procedures and basic child protection (go to **www.scriptureunion.org.uk/holidayclubs** for more information). If your church has a coordinator for this, they should be able to help out at this point. Alternatively, contact CCPAS (The Churches' Child Protection Advisory Service) or visit their website: **www.ccpas.co.uk**.

Leading a small group
Leading a small group of children is a vital part of *Space Academy*. Lieutenants will be the ones who get to know and build relationships with the children, in their small group Starbases. Sometimes these relationships can develop into long-term friendships. Understanding how these groups work and having a set of guidelines are really important.

Small-group role play
If you have a fairly confident group of leaders, try this role-play activity. Six or seven leaders play typical children in a group, and one leader is the Lieutenant. This small group is going to look at the *Star Sheets* activity from Day 1 (see page 38). Split your team into groups of seven or eight, and make sure you provide enough sets of the character descriptions (see below) and everything that you need for the *Star Sheets* activity.

Give out the character descriptions and tell the teams not to show anyone their piece of paper but to act it out during the activity as best they can. Encourage the team not to overact and make their group leader's role a total nightmare, but to take it as seriously as they can.

- You are the Lieutenant. Your group has lots of needs, and you should try very hard to include everyone in the discussion and keep the discussion on track!
- You are an intelligent child who knows all the answers and keeps putting their hand up to answer, or to ask a question, but you don't call out or interrupt.
- You are a very shy younger child, who will be very slow in interacting with the group.
- You are a fidgeter who can't keep still, yet is following what is being discussed.
- You are a child who naturally interrupts all the time, but should respond to firm handling by your Lieutenant. You should ask to go to the toilet at least once during the short group time.
- You are an average sort of child, who is interested in the teaching and discussion. You have got a bit of a crush on your leader, so go and sit next to them if you can and maintain eye contact.
- You listen well and follow all that your leader asks you to do, making a valuable contribution to the group.
- You are deeply committed to Jesus and yet find it very difficult to articulate how you feel or what to say. You try very hard to contribute to the group.

Feedback from the role play
The activity should be a good, fun way of raising some of the issues involved in leading a small group. Have some flip chart paper and markers ready to note down any interesting points to come from the groups.

Talk first to the Lieutenant, encouraging them that at *Space Academy* it will never be as difficult as the last few minutes! Ask them to outline the characters in their group. What was difficult to deal with? Who contributed? Who didn't contribute and why?

Discuss some of the issues raised by the characters, eg, What are you going to do about the child who always asks to go to the toilet? How should you handle leader crushes?

By the time the feedback has finished you should have a set of guidelines for leading a group. Below are a few dos and don'ts which may be worth adding to discussion at the end.

Dos and don'ts of leading a small group
- Do learn the children's names and call them by name.
- Do take notice of how each child behaves, reacts and interacts so you can get to know each one quickly.
- Do take the initiative. Let them know clearly what you expect from the group, how each one is valued and encouraged to participate in the life of the group.
- Do be specific in your prompting and questions (this can help everyone contribute).
- Do try to meet the children's needs (each child will come with their own needs).
- Don't assume that all the children will learn from or experience the club in the same way.
- Do be polite and patient (even if one or two children really annoy you!).
- Do add oodles of enthusiasm to your group (they will pick up on your attitude – you are a role model).
- Do think creatively, eg, how you sit, lie or kneel as a group to discuss things. One way would be for everyone in the group (including leaders) to lie on

the floor on their tummies in a circle with heads in to the centre.
- Do model what you expect the children to do, eg, responding with enthusiasm to the drama!
- Do be careful to follow closely any instructions or notes you are given.
- Do ask for help if you need it (you are not alone!).
- Do be careful with language (no jargon, complicated or inappropriate language).
- Do pray for the children and yourself as you lead the group.
- Don't make favourites.
- Don't be physical with them (this can be misinterpreted).

Here are a few extra thoughts about keeping control to guide you:

The key to establishing good discipline and control is relationship building and clear expectations – these need to be thought through before *Space Academy* starts. This can be done by:
- Setting some ground rules and boundaries for the group – and sticking to them!
- Having plenty of materials for everyone.
- Ensuring you are fully prepared with everything you need to hand. Failure in this can open the door for behaviour problems!
- Ensuring that you have enough leaders at all times.
- Positively reinforcing the children's behaviour when they answer or do something well.
- Never sacrificing the needs of the group for one child.

For more information on leading small groups, check out *Top Tips on Leading small groups* (Scripture Union 978 1 84427 388 1 £2.99).

For more information on managing behaviour, see *Mega Top Tips: Dealing with Challenging Behaviour* (Scripture Union 978 1 84427 531 1 £4.99).

Praying with children
There will be many chances to pray with the children during *Space Academy*. There are two different aspects that come up during *Space Academy*: praying about things with the children and helping them make a response. There will be more about the latter in session 2.

Praying with children
- Ask the children to name some of the things they want to pray for.
- Break these down into things they want to say sorry for, things they want to say thank you to God for, and things they want to ask for themselves or others.
- If you are going to lead the prayer yourself, make sure that you keep to the point and include the suggestions the children made.
- Encourage the children, where possible, to lead the prayers with you.
- Be imaginative in using different ways to pray, eg, using pictures or objects to stimulate thought; music to help praise or reflection; prayers with a set response; taking it in turns using one sentence; or prayers using different bodily postures. Suggestions are given each day for praying creatively.
- Take care to use simple, clear modern English, free from jargon, keeping it brief and relevant.

Talking with God should be very natural and the children need to realise this. Explain that we say 'Amen' as a means of saying we agree. We don't have to close our eyes and put our hands together!

For more information on praying with children, check out *Top Tips on Prompting prayer* (Scripture Union 978 1 84427 322 5 £3.50).

Reading the Bible with children
At *Space Academy* we want the children to understand that the Bible is God's Word for them today. It is important that the times when you read the Bible together are enjoyable and make sense to them! We don't simply read the Bible to get answers to our questions. Instead, we want their curiosity raised so that they can expect to meet God as they read the Bible, not just now, but in the future.

Encourage your team to look at the Bible through the eyes of a child whenever they read it. What would a child find hard? What would they enjoy? What would they be most likely to remember from the passage? Just as children see the world at a different physical level, they often see spiritual things differently too, so encourage everyone to think from a child's perspective.

Prayer
End your session with prayer for *Space Academy*. Draw a large 'gingerbread' child on a sheet of paper; give out sticky notes and pens to everyone and invite them to write prayers on them that are about asking God to help you deal with the specific situations you

have considered in this session: the programme, working with small groups, reading the Bible and praying with children. Then invite everyone to come in turn and stick their prayers on the shape, and to pray briefly either silently or aloud for those things.

Session 2
Talking with children about tough times

You will need: 'Happy days' sheets (make your own on a sheet of A4 paper with a list of 8 to 10 'happy events' that people may have experienced in childhood, such as birthday, Christmas, first bike, trip to the zoo, etc, with space alongside each for people to sign their name), pens; paper; Bibles.

Welcome
Welcome your team with refreshments, and have one of the *Space Academy* theme songs playing in the background.

Introductory activity
Give everyone a 'Happy days' sheet; the object is to have as many different people sign it against something that was a happy day for them in childhood. People can only sign for one event. Encourage the team to achieve this by asking 'Did you …?' rather than simply pushing the sheet in front of the person and asking them to sign whichever they can!

Talk briefly afterwards about any other particularly happy events, picking up on how readily we talk about them.

Daniel in the hot seat
Divide people into up to six groups and give each group a Bible, pen and paper. They should divide the paper with a line down the middle, and on one side write 'happy' and on the other 'tough'. Allocate a different chapter of Daniel 1–6 to each group and ask them to read it together, noting on the paper the things that were happy and those that were tough.

Come together and briefly review the events you have selected. Where was the balance for Daniel: happy or tough?

Ask someone to take on the role of Daniel and sit in the 'hot seat' to be asked questions about one or two tough times (it will need to be someone who knows the stories quite well). Choose two people to act as observers and let the others ask questions of 'Daniel' about the events.

When this has been done, ask the observers what they noticed about the types of questions asked: were they simply factual or did they probe a little into emotions? How did 'Daniel' react to the different types of questions? Which got to the heart of the events? Did any cause particular hurt?

Up to date
It is highly likely that some of the children who come to *Space Academy* will also have faced tough times. Draw up a list together of the sorts of things that may have happened (eg, bereavement, the impact of divorce, bullying etc).

How might you respond if a child talked about one of these events with you? Create a list of dos and don'ts for talking with children who have been through tough times. For example, don't probe – allow the child to bring up the topic; don't leave a child upset; don't **promise** to keep confidences (in case a child should disclose that they are being abused), but **do** keep things confidential unless there is a real need to involve someone else; do be natural and matter-of-fact if they tell you something which shocks you, but don't trivialise things; etc.

This would be a good time to go over your child protection policy and remind people of the action to take if a child should disclose that they are being abused.

Prayer
End this part of the session by praying for any children who are coming to the club that you know are in the midst of difficult times, or who have gone through tough things. Be sure that nothing is included 'for prayer' that is not already public knowledge; be sensitive to details that should be kept private. Ask God to give everyone skill in listening.

Further reading
The Strong Tower (Scripture Union 978 1 84427 122 1 £7.99) is a book of retold Bible stories for tough times, and includes some helpful questions and advice on talking with children.

Helping children to respond
Much of the material you will cover in *Space Academy* may prompt children to want to be friends with God or Jesus for themselves. Be ready to help them, but make sure that you stay within your church's child protection policy when praying with children.

- Unless you bring up the subject, a child may not have the words to begin a conversation with them about responding to Jesus. Explain that if at any time they do want to talk to you more, they should say 'Tell me more about Jesus', and then you will know what they want to discuss.

- They rarely need long explanations, just simple answers to questions.
- Talk to them in a place where you can be seen by others.
- Never put pressure on children to respond in a particular way, just help them take one step closer to Jesus when they are ready. We don't want them to respond just to please us!
- Treat each as an individual. So don't say, 'Hands up who wants to follow Jesus?' or make children say something that is not true for them, but allow each one to choose what is right for them.
- Always allow children a way out: give them an opportunity to go away and think about their decision and come back to you either later in the session or on the following day. This is God's work, and even if you don't have the chance to talk to them again he can actually achieve it without you!
- Remember, many children move through a number of stages of commitment to Jesus as their understanding grows.
- Many children just need a bit of help to say what they want to say to God. Here is a suggested prayer they could use to express their belief in Jesus and desire to belong to him:

> Jesus, I want to be your friend.
> Thank you that you love me.
> Thank you for living in the world
>   and dying on a cross for me.
> I'm sorry for all the wrong things
>   I have done.
> Please forgive me and let me be
>   your friend.
> Please let the Holy Spirit help me
>   be like you.
> Amen.

- Reassure them that God hears us when we talk with him and has promised to forgive us and help us to be his friends. Children need help to stick with Jesus, especially if their parents and/or others around them don't believe.
- Assure them that God wants to hear whatever they say. Give them some prayer ideas.
- Encourage them to keep coming to Christian activities, not necessarily on Sundays – their church might have to be the midweek club or a school lunch-time club.
- Reading the Bible will be easier with something like *Snapshots through the Year* or *Snapshots 365!* – but you need to support them if they are to keep it up.
- Keep praying and maintain your relationship with them wherever possible.

Friends with Jesus (for 5 to 7s), *Me+Jesus* (for 8s and 9s) and *Jesus=friendship forever* (for 10 to 12s) will help to explain what it means to follow Jesus. Details are on the inside front cover.

For more information on helping children respond, see *Top Tips on Helping a child respond to Jesus* (Scripture Union 978 1 84427 387 4 £2.99).

Working with special or additional needs

During *Space Academy* you will face a number of challenges. Being prepared to take care of children with special or additional needs can be a tremendous blessing to both the children and their parents or carers. Here are a few guidelines for working with children with additional needs.

- Value every child as an individual. Before the start, find out as much as possible about them – their likes and dislikes, strengths and limitations. Then you will know how best to include them and make them feel safe.
- Prepare each session with a range of abilities in mind. Think carefully about working with abstract ideas. These may be misunderstood and taken literally! Offer a range of craft ideas. Check that you do not give a child with learning difficulties a task that is appropriate for their reading age but inappropriate for their actual age. In other words, make sure that pictures and other aids are age-appropriate.
- Give all children opportunities to join in activities. Some children with additional needs may have distinctive areas of interest or talents that you can respond to. As far as possible, keep children with disabilities with their own peer group.
- If you have a child with a hearing impairment, make sure they sit near the front and that they can see the speaker's face clearly (not lit from behind). If a loop system is available, check that it is working for the child. Discussion in small groups can be hard for deaf children. Try to reduce background noise.
- Pay attention to any medical needs noted on the registration forms, particularly any medication the children take. Keep a record of any medication given, initialled by the first-aider and another team member.

- Designate leaders to work one-to-one with children with challenging behaviour. Where appropriate, set up a buddy system so that they work closely with a peer.
- Expect good behaviour from all children, but be tolerant of unusual behaviour. For example, some children need to fiddle with something in their hands. 'Concentrators' can be bought from **www.tangletoys.com**.
- Ensure that all the children know what is planned for the day. Some children will benefit from a schedule in words or symbols. Give the children a five-minute countdown when an activity is about to finish. Some children find any change of activity very difficult.

Top tips on Welcoming special children (Scripture Union 978 1 84427 126 9 £3.50)

Helping children with special needs to know God is challenging, but deeply rewarding. Find out what the Bible has to say on the subject and explore the implications of the Disability Discrimination Act for your church. Be encouraged and inspired with stories from group leaders and parents, and be equipped with lots of practical ideas for welcoming special children to your church and children's group.

Working with children from other faith backgrounds

Having children from different faiths come to our events is a great privilege. Knowing that their parents trust us to care for their children and are willing to allow us to share the Good News of Jesus is exciting, but also gives us a responsibility to think about how we are going to treat the children and relate to their faith and culture. The principles below have been worked out by practitioners with many years' experience of working in this context. Whilst you might not agree with all of them we think they are worth serious consideration in order to ensure that we give a genuine welcome to children from other faith backgrounds. We have written these recognising that whilst some parents from different faiths are keen for their children to attend a club run by Christians, they might still have strong objections to their children becoming followers of Jesus. It is with this and other tensions in mind that we have produced these principles.

- We will not criticise, ridicule or belittle other religions.
- We will not tell the children what their faith says, nor define it by what some of its adherents do.
- We will not ask the children to say, sing or pray things that they do not believe, understand or that compromise their own faith.
- We will value and affirm the positive aspects of the children's culture.
- We will use music, artwork and methods that are culturally appropriate, for example Asian Christian music, pictures of people from a variety of backgrounds or single-sex activities.
- We will be open and honest in our presentation of what Christians believe.
- We will be open and honest about the aims and content of our work with families, carers, teachers and other adults involved in their lives.
- We will seek to build long-term friendships that are genuine and which have no hidden agendas.
- We will relate to the children and young people within the context of their families and their families' belief system.
- We are committed to the long-term nature of the work, for the children now and the impact this could have on future generations.
- Where children show a desire to follow Jesus we will discuss the issues surrounding such a course of action, particularly relating to honouring and obeying parents. We will be honest about the consequences following Jesus might have for them.
- We will never suggest that the children keep things secret from their families or carers.
- We seek to promote mutual respect between diverse groups and encourage community cohesion.

Top Tips on Welcoming children of other faiths (Scripture Union 978 1 84427 250 1 £3.50)

What does the Bible say about those of other faiths and how we should live out our faith amongst them? What can your church do? Here's a readable and practical guide which will inspire and equip you to build relationships with children and their families. It's packed with practical, fun ideas that will strengthen or even kick-start your ministry with those of other faiths.

If you expect to have children from other faith backgrounds attending, remind your team of the importance of treating the Bible as a holy book: never simply put it down on the floor, but always place it carefully on a table (and especially don't use it to raise the height of a projector, for example!). Be sure that you use copies that are in good condition, as one which is falling apart would be shameful to some children from other faith backgrounds.

If you are serving food at any activities, check that it will be appropriate for any child from another faith background.

Prayer

Spend some time together as a team praying for each other, for *Space Academy* and for all the children who will come.

It would be great to get the leaders of each Starbase to pray together. You may wish to use some of the creative prayer ideas you will find in each day's session outlines.

Or find some silhouettes of children, preferably of a boy and a girl, and print off enough for everyone to have one of each. Use the silhouettes to pray for the children who will come: they may be unknown to you, but God knows their names and all their needs. Ask him to be at work in each child. Encourage team to take home their silhouettes and pray for the children regularly. You may even want to turn them in to fridge magnets – print on card and stick magnetic tape on the back – so that they are in a prominent place. (But do not include any child's name on anything that team will take home with them.)

Pray too for the team by having all of those in each role stand whilst you pray for them and their work during *Space Academy*. Ask God to fill each one with his Holy Spirit to make them more like Jesus and to skill them for the tasks he has given them.

Session 3

Listening and talking with children

This training feature is available on the DVD and at **www.scriptureunion.org.uk/spaceacademy** as a paid-for download.

You may also find these *Top Tips* books helpful:

Top Tips on Sharing Bible stories (Scripture Union 978 1 84427 328 7 £3.50)

Top Tips on Communicating God in non-book ways (Scripture Union 978 1 84427 329 4 £3.50)

Top Tips on Discovering the Bible with children (Scripture Union 978 1 84427 335 5 £3.50)

Top Tips on Running holiday clubs (Scripture Union 978 1 84427 541 0 £3.50)

CAPTAIN'S LOG 4

Session outlines

Star dates

Planning your session

When you come to plan each day, make sure you have read the descriptions of the programme in Captain's Log 1. Select the activities according to the children you are likely to have at the club.

You do not need to include all the activities listed here in your programme.

Making your choice

There are many factors which will influence your choice of activities:

The children involved

The children should be the most important consideration when choosing the daily activities. Children respond differently to the same activity. Lieutenants in particular should bear this in mind when planning Lunar landing.

The length of the club

Simply, if you have a long club, then you will be able to do more! The timings given are merely guidelines; different children will take different lengths of time to complete the same activity. Be flexible in your timings, judge whether it would be more valuable to complete an activity, even though it may be overrunning, rather than cut it short and go on to the next activity. Have something in your programme you can drop if things overrun.

The leaders available

Not every club will be able to find leaders with the necessary skills to fulfil every requirement. If you can't find anyone with a Basic Food Hygiene Certificate, you will have to limit the refreshments you can provide. If you don't have musicians, then you'll have to rely on backing tracks or miss out the singing.

To help Lieutenants prepare for Lunar landing, the questions for each day are called 'Bible discovery' and can be found in each day and on the website.

Blast off Sunday service 1
Taken away

Key passage
Daniel 1:1–7

Key storylines
- The people of Israel are taken from their homes to the very different country of Babylon, where no one knows of, or believes in, God.
- Daniel and his three friends are chosen for special training.

Key aims
- To introduce the Bible story of Daniel and the theme of *Space Academy*.
- To explore the background to Daniel and his friends' move to Babylon, why God allowed this to happen and to consider if God was still with them.
- To intrigue children about what will happen to Daniel and his friends and to invite them to the holiday club to find out.

For children with no church background
These children need to be welcomed and helped to enjoy the service. Try to think about what will be unfamiliar to them, like when to stand and when to sit, and what words they may not understand. It's good to make sure that people they know are involved in the service in some way, at least in planning it, preferably in presenting it.

For church children
Encourage church children to look out for their friends who don't usually come, and to sit with them to help them feel part of what is going on. Some church children might help to welcome their friends, or take some part in the service. By involving them you can help them feel part of the holiday club in a special way.

For children of other faiths
If you do have children and their families coming to this first church service, make sure you have people ready to welcome them when they arrive. This may be their first visit to a church so have someone on hand to help them know what to do, to explain what is happening throughout the service and to reassure them that it's OK if they want to just watch and listen rather than join in the singing or praying. At the end, introduce them to other children and families who they could form friendships with. If they are coming to a church service they will expect it to be a Christian act of worship. Don't feel intimidated or that you have to 'water down' the message. But make them feel welcome as they are, not just as you'd like them to be.

The whole theme of moving to a new and foreign land may be very familiar to those who have only just arrived or whose parents came to this country as a child or adult. However, do not presume that this is the case, for there are many who are 'second and third generation' who feel themselves British but from a faith other than Christianity. If you live in an area of mixed faiths and cultures, spend some time researching the demographics of your locality so that you are familiar with who may attend the club.

If you are part of a church that has members who were born abroad and have settled in this country, you may want to invite them to talk about their experiences, especially if others were unable to pronounce their names or ended up anglicising their names. They could also talk about how they felt and relate this to Daniel and his friends.

For children with additional needs
Parents will value your non judgemental acceptance of their child. Ask parents or carers how best to welcome their child as they will not bring their child unless they are confident that their child can be included, encouraged and kept safe.

As you begin to make friends with the child, assume that they are able to understand you. Just because a child cannot speak, move or see does not mean that they do not understand. Each child will want to be treated the same as any other child of the same age.

Service outline

You will need
The Space Academy DVD; a selection of warning road signs (eg, level crossing ahead, danger of grounding, slippery road surface etc) either printed or drawn large enough for people to see, or on OHP or PowerPoint, for the quiz; a sign or PowerPoint slide saying 'What should they do?' for the talk.

Welcome
Welcome everyone and explain that the service may be a little different from your usual style, as it is the launch of *Space Academy*. Talk briefly about the holiday club so everyone is aware of what is happening in the week ahead. It will become clearer through the service why the theme is about space.

Start with a song that celebrates God's awesome and holy nature, or his creation of the world.

Set the scene
Show a clip from Episode 1 of the DVD of the children talking with one of the astrophysicists, and then use the facts in it to lead a prayer of thanks to God for the amazing universe he has created. You could use the prayer below, or invite people to say what they are amazed by, and then lead a prayer in your own words.

Leader: Almighty God, you created the universe in all its splendour: galaxies, stars, planets, constellations, light and dark, night and day. Nothing was made without you, and you hold it all in your hands.

All: Almighty God, you are awesome!

Leader: The light which brightens our day right now left the sun's core 30,000 years ago – yet you were there long before that, and always will be.

All: Almighty God, you are awesome!

Leader: As our earth travels through space, each minute we are 19,000 kilometres away from where we were – and yet we are always with you.

All: Almighty God, you are awesome!

Leader: Our planet is so small that over 1 million earths would fit on the sun, yet you know and care about every individual who lives on earth – who ever has, and ever will.

All: Almighty God, you are awesome!

Leader: Though you are our awesome God, you came to earth to live as a man, in your son Jesus Christ. And through his death and resurrection you made it possible for all who believe in him to be with you forever.

All: Almighty God, you are awesome! Amen.

Introductory activity
This simple quiz will work best if everyone answers every question rather than asking separate questions of each team. Either have teams of mixed ages at the front or simply divide everyone into groups where they are sitting, and for each question choose a different person as spokesperson for their group.

Ask the groups to identify the warning road signs that you show.

Finally, ask the teams to think of as many methods of giving a warning as possible (eg, car horn, fire alarm, etc)

Pick up from that and talk about the warnings God gave people right from the start of this world's life – eg, the command to Adam and Eve not to eat the fruit of the tree of knowledge of good and evil; the Ten Commandments; the words of the prophets telling people not to ignore God but to follow him and his ways. Even now we sometimes ignore God's warnings and do things our way, running into danger by doing so (you might include some relevant examples). Lead a short prayer of confession such as the following prayer.

Leader: Lord God, you are wise and good, giving us rules by which to live. But sometimes we forget and break them, and for that…

All: We are sorry, God.

Leader: Lord God, you are kind and gracious, reminding us when we forget your ways. But sometimes we ignore you, and for that…

All: We are sorry, God.

Leader: Lord God, you are loving and forgiving. Help us day by day to hear your voice, to know your ways and to walk in them.

All: Amen.

Star songs
The Captain should introduce The Transporters band (if you are going to have a band at *Space Academy*) and get them to teach everyone the *Space Academy* theme song of your choice. Once you have sung it through a couple of times, sing some other songs of worship to God. Select ones that your church are familiar with that talk about God's power and how we can trust in him. Remember that you may have people unused to church in your service, so try to avoid any songs with lyrics that will be confusing or that mean they will be singing something that they don't necessarily believe. Here are some suggestions:

- Be Bold, be strong!
  The Source 38
- Father, I place into your hands
  The Source 97
- Holy, holy, holy
  Songs of Fellowship 1281
- Immortal, invisible
  The Source 220
- I'm gonna trust in God
  Songs of Fellowship 1339
- Our God is an awesome God
  The Source 148
- Our God is a great big God
  Songs of Fellowship 2004

Tell the Bible story
Some years before our story begins, God had spoken to a man called Jeremiah, who was living in Jerusalem, and told him that he must warn God's people that they had broken the covenant or agreement with God made many, many years before, by following the gods of their neighbouring countries. God knew that following him was best and he wanted to help his people turn back to him. So, the warning Jeremiah gave stated that if they continued to disobey God, the king of Babylon would sweep into the land with his army, and the people would have a terrible time. How should God's people respond to this message? What should they do? *(show the 'What should they do?' sign)* Ask a few people of different ages what they think God's people should do.

The right thing was to say sorry to God, to trust that he knew best, to stop worshipping the false gods and start following God again. But the people didn't listen to Jeremiah, and they didn't listen to God. Even though God gave them lots of time to change, they didn't. And so, about 40 years later, everything that God had warned his people about happened: the king of Babylon, Nebuchadnezzar, swept into the country with his army, right up to the walls of Jerusalem, and eventually took control of the city and its people. He took many, many people away from Jerusalem back to Babylon. And there, life was as different as if they were living on another planet – hence our space theme! And that's where our story really begins.

At this point in the talk you could re-enact the Israelites going into exile by getting everyone who is able to, to get out of their seats and to walk around the building several times. When everyone is back in place continue with the story as follows.

Amongst the people taken captive was a young man called Daniel, and his friends Hananiah, Mishael and Azariah. They were handsome young men, strong, fit, clever and quick to learn even more things. The king wanted them to be trained in the Babylonian language and life. He gave them new names: Belteshazzar, Shadrach, Meshach and Abednego. All their own names had something of God in them, but these names were linked to pagan gods, and would have made the men very, very sad. So what should they do? *(show the sign again) Ask a few people of different ages what they think Daniel and his friends should do.*

Our names may be very precious to us, but these men somehow decided not to complain, and instead to allow themselves to be called by their new names. I don't know if they believed that God was still watching over them, but they accepted what happened and lived quietly in their new country. For a while…

But then something else happened! The king said they must eat food from his own table: every kind of meat you can think of, including pork. Now Daniel and his friends didn't eat pork; it was one of the laws that God had given them. So what should they do? *(show the sign again)*

Ask a few people of different ages what they think Daniel and his friends should do.

If you want to know what Daniel and his friends did, you'll have to come to *Space Academy* tomorrow, or come back next Sunday to find out! But think about this: when you have decisions to make this week, *(show the sign for a last time)* how will you decide what to do? Will you allow God, his Word the Bible, and his ways, to shape your thinking and your doing?

Prayer

Lead a prayer about the things that people might be doing this week, including *Space Academy* and for situations or people who are in need of God's help, especially those who, through war or political unrest, have been forced to leave their homes and go to another country. Invite people to join in with the response 'Help us to trust you' after each short section. You might show images taken from the internet to illustrate the topics as appropriate.

Star songs

Sing the *Space Academy* song again to finish the service. Make sure all the children know about the first session of the club, and have registration forms on hand so that children can sign up. Give out any information about family events that you're running alongside the club, and about any other appropriate events in your church's programme.

Voyage 1
Forbidden food

Key passage
Daniel 1:8–21

Key storylines
- Daniel, Shadrach, Meshach and Abednego stand firm for God and choose to follow his ways.
- God influences the Babylonian officials to support them and gives the four young men the ability to learn and become wise.

Key aims
- To discover that Daniel and his friends had a choice to make – and that God did not let them down.
- To realise that God helps us when we think about what he wants us to do, and when we do our best to live his way.
- To welcome all the children, start building relationships and have fun together.

For children with no church background
Few children who are new to church will know much about the story of Daniel. The idea of not eating something to obey God will be strange, and they might be amazed that Daniel and his friends would choose vegetables instead of meat. Help them to see that it was all because Daniel followed God, the whole idea of which may never have entered their minds before.

For church children
As soon as you mention Daniel, many church children will be thinking about lions, but they may not know the first part of the story, which we tell today. Of course they know about God, and may know a bit about the Old Testament rules that led Daniel to not eat the king's food. Encourage them to tell you what they know about this, especially when you are in groups. They will probably not really know that Daniel and his friends are miles away from home, and quite likely scared about what is happening to them.

For children of other faiths
This passage will be very easy for all children from other faith backgrounds to relate to as almost all other faith groups have food that is forbidden to eat. It would therefore be appropriate to ask the children if there is anything that they cannot eat or at times refrain from eating. Because different groups may adhere to different rules, do not presume you know what these foods are but ask the children to explain what they can or cannot eat. Do not be upset if they refer to food that they can't eat as 'Christian food' for it's sometimes assumed that Britain is a Christian country and therefore that the food eaten here is also Christian.

For children with additional needs
This may be the first time a child has attended something like a holiday club. Starting something new will feel like a potential threat to a child with an autistic spectrum disorder (ASD) or attention deficit hyperactive disorder (ADHD). A schedule of activities will encourage confident, calm behaviour. It's all about relationships. Make sure each child knows who will help and where to go for time out (maybe a beanbag in a corner).

Some children with additional needs may have a restricted diet because certain foods may cause a choking hazard or exacerbate their medical condition. It may be a good time to explain to other children in the group that, kind as it is to share snacks and sweets, it would be better not to because some people have food allergies. But do this in a way that doesn't draw too much attention to any particular child. Be sure to check registration forms for allergies!

VOYAGE 1 **FORBIDDEN FOOD**

Lieutenants' briefing

Spiritual preparation

Read together
Read Daniel 1:8–21 and outline the threads of the Bible story.

Explore together
This part of the narrative may be unfamiliar to the team as well as the children. Briefly summarise the rules that God gave his people from Leviticus 11 and Deuteronomy 14:1–21. The likelihood was that the king's diet would include foods forbidden to God's people. Today, most of God's people are happy to eat all kinds of foods – if children ask about this look at Mark 7:17–19 and Acts 10:14,15.

Run through the aims for the day (those listed on page 32 and others that you have chosen for the club), and think through and chat informally about how these are going to be met through the time together.

Reflect together
The key reason why Daniel refused the food was that it would make him ritually unclean, and he wanted to keep his relationship with God pure. What things mar our relationship with God? At the start of the club, take time to be quiet with God and ask his forgiveness for anything that might keep you from hearing God today.

By keeping to God's rules in this apparently minor way, Daniel and his friends made a stand. God showed his support to them in this – which may well have given them the confidence to trust him in the much greater challenges that were to come. What things strengthen our relationship with God? Share any examples from your own experience where you have been able to trust God because he has been your support in the past. As a team, you are about to launch into the club: you can be confident in God, because he has shown his power and trustworthiness before to you and to others.

Pray together
Pray that the children will feel really welcomed, will really enjoy themselves and will get excited about coming. Once they're excited about holiday club, it is a shorter journey to get excited about the God at the centre of it. Pray for each other, for good relationships within the team, for stamina, boldness, patience and to be good examples to the children.

Practical preparation

Talk through your programme together, remind everyone of the programme and who is doing what, ensuring that everyone knows their part in the day and has everything they need. Pay special attention to younger leaders and helpers or those who have not taken part in your holiday club before: give them an extra boost of encouragement.

Set up the different areas of the club and make sure that everything is in place in plenty of time, so you are ready as the first children come from the registration area.

Listen to any last-minute information or instructions from your Fleet admiral.

Encourage the team to greet children who came to the first service (if you held one) and welcome everyone, especially those for whom this is the first time they have ever come to anything run by your church.

Share a 'team booster' before heading into the club. (For example, stand closely in a circle, with one arm out and touching hands with everyone else; say together 'Be bold, be strong, for the Lord our God is with us.')

Remember to smile!

What you need checklist

- **Registration** Registration forms, badges, labels, pens, team lists
- **Starbases** Bibles, *Daniel's Data* or *Star Sheets*, Bible discovery notes
- **Music** The Transporters band or backing tracks
- **Drama** Costumes and props
- **Technology** PA system, laptop, PowerPoints and projection/OHP and acetates, *Space Academy* DVD
- **Activities** Equipment for games and construction
- **The Captain** Running order, notes, Full throttle and One giant leap equipment, quiz questions and globe
- **The Space Commander** Story script, props for the story
- **Café Cosmos** Drinks and biscuits or other refreshments

Space programme

As the children arrive and register, play some space-related or sci-fi music (such as *Star Trek*, *Star Wars* or *Dr Who*) and display the *Space Academy* logo on the screen to welcome the children.

As this is the first main day of the club, make sure the registration team is ready to greet and register the children, so that any new children and parents don't have to wait long. Have a welcome team on hand to take the children to their groups. Encourage Lieutenants and Ensigns to be ready to welcome the children in their groups, tell them where the toilets are, etc.

Report to starbase

10 minutes
small groups

Starbase mobile

What you need
- Each letter of your Starbase name – eg, Mercury – written on different coloured sheets of card in 'bubble' writing and cut out
- Planet or star shapes cut out of card
- Wool or ribbon
- Felt pens or stickers
- Bead

What you do
Welcome the children to *Space Academy* and ask each one their name. Show them the name of your Starbase and let each child choose a letter to write their own name on and to decorate with felt pens or stickers. Have a few extra planet or star shapes for quick finishers or if you have a large group of children. Tape the letters in order down a length of wool or ribbon, making a loop at the top and including any extra shapes before or after

CAPTAIN'S LOG 4

your Starbase name. Hang a bead at the end if you wish. Read down the children's names, asking them to stand up and turn round when their name is announced. Hang the Starbase mobile in your area.

Action stations!

45 minutes all together

Bring everyone together so that the astronauts can get active! Play the *Space Academy* theme song as a sign for the children to join the larger group.

The Captain should introduce themselves and welcome everyone to *Space Academy*. They should run through the day's programme briefly and tell everyone where the toilets are and what to do in the event of a fire. Set out any simple rules that you have for the club. Introduce the space capsule, where astronauts can leave jokes, pictures and questions. Let the children know that they will have the opportunity to interview one of the team later, so get them to think of questions they would like to ask.

Phaser-fitness

Super Nova reminds the astronauts of their need for exercise on board the spaceship so that they are fit for anything that happens. Play suitable space-themed music (eg *Star Trek* or *Dr Who* title music) and create some exercises to do with eating – eg, digging up vegetables, peeling potatoes, cutting carrots, stirring a stew, raising hand to mouth to eat.

Brain boosters

The Captain introduces Buzz Brain. He could ask him what he studied at university and he could reply with some long-winded unpronounceable qualification such as a doctorate in Stellar-astro-geophysical-density-fusion-magnetosphere-cosmology. The Captain looks suitably impressed and then asks Buzz what he had for breakfast. He replies '237.67534 grammes of sprouts' (hopefully you'll get some response to this)! The Captain goes on to say that in today's story they'll be hearing more about training and food. 'But first, what can you tell us about space food and the Astronaut Training Programme, Buzz?'

Buzz then shares the following facts:

1. The first food eaten in space was apple sauce packed into something like a toothpaste tube – not that appetising! Now astronauts eat most things that we do on earth such as mashed potatoes, chocolate pudding and tortillas. Food is freeze-dried so it can be kept for a long time – astronauts just add hot water! (You can get packs of freeze-dried food from Amazon or from outdoor pursuit shops so, if you like, you could supply a live demo.) Snacks like cereal bars or nuts are fun to eat. Just open the packet and let the nut or piece of bar float into your mouth!

2. All astronauts undergo years of intensive training – usually 13 years after leaving school. Here are some essential requirements:
   - Good grades at school and university in Maths and Science
   - Excellent eyesight and fitness levels
   - For astronaut pilots, 1,000 hours of pilot-in-command time in a jet aircraft
   - Pass a swimming test that involves swimming three lengths of a 25-metre pool without stopping, and then do it again in a flight suit and tennis shoes.

Full throttle

Zero-gravity dining

What you need
- Various soft food
- Spoons
- Tables and chairs
- Cover-up and clean-up equipment

What you do
Ask for pairs of volunteers (more than one pair, if you have enough space). Give one of each pair a covering for their clothes, sit them on a chair at a table and ask them to put their hands behind their back. Ask the other in the pair to stand behind them and put their arms through the seated person's arms (so that they can reach any items on the table). Place your choice of soft food in front of each pair, and tell the person at the back that they have to feed their partner! This is to help them get the hang of eating food in zero gravity. The winner is the pair to finish their food first.

Star songs

Introduce The Transporters band (if you have one) and get them to teach the *Space Academy* theme song of your choice and any actions, if you've come up with some. Sing it a couple of times so that the astronauts begin to get the hang of it, rather than singing other songs at this point. Say that you'll sing it again later!

One giant leap

This activity ties into the Bible passage as it introduces the idea of food, and what we do and don't like to eat.

Space rations

What you need
- Various soft foods in bowls/cups (eg, baby food, egg custard, mushy peas, rice pudding, fruit puree, chocolate spread, fish spread, jam, etc)
- Blindfolds
- Spoons
- Clean-up and cover-up facilities

What you do
Ask for volunteers (one from each group). Help each volunteer put on a blindfold. Feed each volunteer the food in turn and ask them to identify each one. Give points for correct guesses! Try to include a variety of flavours and textures.

Be aware of food allergy issues and religious sensitivities when playing this game.

Tell the story

For each Voyage, there are three options suggested for telling the Bible story: you can use the same approach each time, mix and match how you tell the story, or combine two or more approaches. Choose which will be most helpful for your team, your children and the style of your club.

1. The Space Commander now goes on to tell the Bible story based on Daniel 1:8–21, using their own words if possible (see page 7 for tips on how to do this). You can use the section headings, props

and actions from the script (see option 3) as memory joggers and to vary your story presentation each time.

2. Introduce today's episode from the *Space Academy* DVD. (If you are telling the story and using the DVD, tell the story first, then show the DVD so the children already have the outline of the events before seeing the episode.)

3. Or the Space Commander may prefer to follow the fully scripted retold Bible story for Voyage 1 on page 72.

Using props

Give the children plenty of opportunity to interact and provide them with suitable props. You will need name tags for Daniel, Shadrach, Meshach and Abednego, large pictures of burgers mounted on to cardboard or play food items and a selection of four different vegetables. If you're creative you may like to make giant versions of the vegetables so everyone can see what the volunteers are holding.

Universe challenge

The Captain should thank the Space Commander and then introduce the quiz. Before the session, put together some questions about the Bible story and also include the space and astronaut facts Buzz Brain gave earlier. You could include:

- What was the first food eaten in space?
- Name one requirement for being an astronaut?
- What food did Daniel and his friends eat?
- Name one requirement the king had to become a court official.

Make the quiz quick and lively, so the children have a chance to review the story and let off some steam after sitting and listening. For today's scoring system, have a globe. Allocate a number from one to six for each continent of the world. For example: Antarctica 1; Africa 2; Asia 3; Europe 4; The Americas 5; Australia 6. If a child answers a question correctly, get them to come up and lightly spin the globe. After a few seconds, get them to close their eyes and stop the globe by leaving their finger on a particular place. Allocate the score according to the continent (or closest continent to) where their finger lands.

Data check

Using the points below, spend a few moments summing up the teaching for the day.

- God's people were in a strange new land where no one knew of, or believed in, God.
- Daniel, Shadrach, Meshach and Abednego had a choice to make – and God did not let them down.
- They stood firm for God and chose to follow his ways even when that meant being a bit different– like eating only vegetables!
- For us, too, following God often means we are different from others or do things differently (give some examples like not swearing, telling the truth, refusing to join in with gossip, etc).
- Because Daniel and his friends trusted God, he gave them the ability to learn and become wise.
- God helps us, too, when we think about what he wants us to do, and when we do our best to live his way.
- Through it all, Daniel and his friends discovered that they hadn't left God behind – he was still with them and helped them.
- When we move to a new place or go to a new school, we don't leave God behind either – he promises to be with us always.

Prayer

To conclude Action Stations! you may want to pause here to give the children an opportunity to think about what they've learnt and to pray silently. Before the session, create a 'space' prayer action that you can do just before you pray. You could say something like, 'Start to think about what God is like from what you've heard in this story – what would you want to say to him, right now? Because you can do that right now!' Make this time short as the children will probably only be quiet for a minute or so. Say 'Amen' or have another action so everyone knows it is the end of the prayer.

Lunar landing

45 minutes small groups

During this time, remind the leaders to collect any questions for On the star spot and get them to the person being interviewed in plenty of time.

Cafe Cosmos

In groups, have your refreshments together (raw vegetables such as carrots, sliced peppers or cauliflower florets would be good), and chat about the club so far. What are the children's favourite parts? Remind your Starbase group to think of questions for On the star spot to put in the space capsule, along with their jokes and pictures. Today's jokes could be on the theme of vegetables.

Bible discovery

With older children (8–10s)

Remind the children that Daniel and his friends were taken from their home town of Jerusalem, 800 km away to Babylon. Get them to work out the route they took on the map on page 6 of *Daniel's Data*. See if you can work out together where you'd be if you were taken 800 km from home. Talk together about what you would miss if you were taken away from your home town, village or city and get the children to write or draw their ideas on page 7. Go on to read Daniel 1:8–14 (either from the Bible or on page 8) and get the children to underline the words in the passage that tell them why Daniel and his friends wanted to only eat vegetables.

Encourage the children to answer the questions on pages 9 and 10. Talk about whether they expected Daniel and his friends to look healthier and better than the men who'd had the king's food.

Read about Daniel and his friends' training from Daniel 1:17–21 on page 11. Get the children to crack the code to find out what the men had to be like in order to do the training.

Talk about how Daniel, Shadrach, Meshach and Abednego chose to stand firm for God and followed his ways. Make sure they understand that although it may not seem that important – it was just about what they ate – it was a risky thing for them to do. When they chose God's way he did not let them down. Ask the children what this tells them about God. Ask them if they think God will help them when they think about what he wants them to do and when they do their best to live his way.

With younger children (5–7s)
Remind the children of the fact that the people of God were in a foreign land, a long way from home. Say how the king wanted all the men he'd chosen to train as court officials to eat the king's food. Read Daniel 1:8–16 using a child-friendly Bible or retell it with your own words (but have a Bible with you so that children know where the story comes from). Look at the pictures together on *Star Sheet 1*. Encourage the children to circle the things Daniel and his friends could eat. Chat about the food they like to eat and encourage them to colour these in on the sheet. Respond by writing the thank you prayer.

Colour in the Xs and Ys to read the message: God will help me do what is right and good. Talk about why it was important for the men to do what was right by only eating vegetables. Think together about the things we need to do which are right and good.

Chat together about things the children might want to pray about, and tell them of a time when God helped you to do something right and good. Spend some time praying together.

With all ages
Adapt these questions to suit your group, sharing your own feelings, opinions and experiences as appropriate:
- Has anyone ever been somewhere very different from their home town? What things were different about it?
- How do you think Daniel felt as one of the few people in the king's palace who believed in God?
- Do you think it helped that Daniel and his friends all decided to stand firm? Would it have been harder for Daniel on his own? If so, how?
- If you'd been with Daniel do you think you would only have eaten vegetables? Why/Why not? (Be clear that this was not about becoming a vegetarian but about doing what God wanted. They could not be sure that the meat was the sort that God had said they could eat so they asked not to eat any.)
- What have you learnt about God from today's Bible story?
- Is it sometimes hard for you to know how to live God's way? How might God want to help you today?

Shuttlecraft
Choose a construction activity from page 68. For extra craft ideas, see *Ultimate Craft* (SU, 978 1 84427 364 5).

Fit for space
Check that your astronauts are fit for space by choosing a games activity from page 70. For extra games ideas, see *Ultimate Games* (SU, 978 1 84427 365 2).

Red alert
25 minutes all together

Space capsule
Welcome everyone back together by playing the *Space Academy* theme song. If there are any messages in the space capsule, read one or two out now. As today is the first day have some pre-prepared to give the children the idea, such as:

Knock, Knock
Who's there? Lettuce
Lettuce Who?
Lettuce in and you'll find out!

Remind the astronauts to bring in jokes and pictures tomorrow.

Star songs
Have The Transporters lead two or three songs that are easy to pick up or have some funny actions. Choose ones that will engage children who aren't used to singing.

Data recall
The Captain rounds up what the Starbases have been exploring together, recapping the following points:
- Daniel and his friends stood up for their faith. In their strange new land, they lived as God's friends and followed his ways, despite being different.
- God didn't let them down – he gave them wisdom and understanding.
- When we choose to follow God, he helps us and promises to be with us always.

Cosmic code
Introduce the Learn and remember verse for *Space Academy* for the week: Proverbs 3:5,6. Talk a bit about how Daniel and his friends had to trust God and not rely on what they thought themselves. Say how this is an important verse for us to take notice of today.

If you are using the Learn and remember song, start to teach it to the children. The sheet music for this can be found on page 88.

Split the amount to learn into two parts: learn verse five today and tomorrow and verse 6 and the Bible reference on days three and four. On day 5 you can put the whole thing together. Before today's session, write the words on several balloons using a permanent marker. Muddle up the order and ask for some volunteers to come to the front to put the balloons in the right order and hold them up. Everyone reads out the verse. Your volunteers tap the balloons in the air a few times, catch them and sort the words out again. Say the verse together again. Gradually remove the balloons until you've all learnt the verse.

If you prefer to have a different verse each day, you will find suggestions for this on the *Space Academy* website.

On the star spot
This is a time in the holiday club to talk about Jesus and the possibility of relationship with him, naturally and simply. Daniel followed the God he knew – but we can know more than he did because we can know Jesus. Interview one of the Lieutenants or Ensigns about a time when they had to go somewhere that was new and felt very different, and how they were helped by the knowledge that Jesus was with them.

VOYAGE 1 **FORBIDDEN FOOD**

Be direct! God did not let Daniel down: ask the interviewee if their experience was that Jesus did not let them down when they trusted him.

Also include the question you have picked out from those the children thought of and invite them to come up and ask it to the interviewee. When they have finished answering, give the 'prize' to the child and thank the Lieutenant or Ensign for being On the star spot!

Drama: The final frontier

Introduce the comedy-drama, 'The final frontier'. It's a big day for Captain Kim and the crew of the Starship (insert name of your club/town) as they await their mission instructions from Mission Command. But something or someone is trying to stop their plans from being successful.

Final orbit

Round off Red alert! by asking the children what they have enjoyed at *Space Academy* today and then include those things in a short prayer of thanks, using your space prayer action, if you came up with one. Encourage the children to come back tomorrow by saying something similar to the following:

'Well we've been on an amazing voyage today but this is just the start. What will the effect of all those sprouts be on Buzz Brain? Will Daniel, Shadrach, Meshach and Abednego continue to stand firm, when the people around them don't believe in their God? Will Spot have mastered the language of Zingyping and will you astronauts stand up to Super Nova's gruelling Phaser-fitness routine? Don't miss out – come back to *Space Academy* tomorrow to find out!'

Sing the *Space Academy* theme song and send the astronauts back to their Starbases to round off the day's session.

Touchdown

10 minutes
small groups

Creative prayer

Look together at the Starbase mobile you made earlier. Take turns to think of a fruit or vegetable beginning with one of the letters in the name of the Starbase. Let this lead you into remembering together the key points of today's teaching.

Look at the mobile again. This time take turns to thank God for one of the other children in the group (you can use the names on the mobile to jog your memory!). As leader, finish with a thank you for any children who were not mentioned by the others. Encourage the children to come back for the next session and to bring their friends.

Voyage clear-up

30 minutes
team time

After all the children have gone, clear up from the day's events and set up for the next session, if the premises you are using makes that feasible. Meet together as a team to debrief. Use a feedback system that works best for you – there is an evaluation form on the *Space Academy* website. This would be the time for the Fleet admiral to raise any obvious issues such as an instant improvement to the registration queue or similar. Also raise anything that has cropped up that needs sorting before tomorrow and assign someone to sort it out. Remember to praise the team for the things that went well and urge them to do as well or better tomorrow! Have a brief time of prayer where Lieutenants and Ensigns can pray for their groups, and other team members can pray for their areas of responsibility. If you have the time and the facilities, you may wish to share a meal together.

CAPTAIN'S LOG 4

SPACE ACADEMY

PHOTOCOPIABLE PAGE

Star sheet Voyage 1
Forbidden food

Bible fun with a friend or on your own.

1 Daniel and his friends only ate fruit and vegetables. Circle the things **they** could eat. Colour in the ones **you** like.

2 Write or draw a thank you prayer to God for your favourite food.

3 Colour in every square with an X or Y to read the message.

x	G	y	o	d	x	x	w	i	y	l	y	l	h	x	e	y	l
p	x	m	y	e	y	d	x	o	w	x	h	y	a	t	x	i	s
r	i	y	g	x	h	t	x	a	n	y	d	g	y	o	o	x	d

TRAINEE'S LOG 1

Voyage 2
The difficult dream

Key passages
Daniel 2:1–6,12–19,31–49

Key storylines
- King Nebuchadnezzar has a dream and is ready to kill all his advisers if they cannot tell him both the dream and its meaning.
- God gives Daniel the secret of the dream, in answer to prayer.
- Daniel tells the king the dream and its interpretation and he, Shadrach, Meshach and Abednego are promoted to high positions in the government of Babylon.

Key aim
- To hear how God gave Daniel the ability to do something that no one else could do and discover why King Nebuchadnezzar declared that God is 'above all other gods and kings'.
- To learn that God helps and protects his friends.
- To continue to build relationships with the children and welcome those who are new to the club today.

Further aim
- To explore the meaning of the king's dream, in the light of what we know about Jesus.

For children with no church background
This story has it all: mystery, tension, drama, a last-minute reprieve and a real surprise as the God of heaven gives Daniel the secret of the mystery dream just at the right time. It's the sort of story that reminds you of some children's fiction, so be sure to point out that we are talking about a true story from the Bible.

For church children
Church children may know this story a little, though they may get confused over some of the dream stories, so don't assume they have it all clear. One problem church children might have (and adults for that matter) is that we don't see much of this sort of thing happening in our churches today – so is the God of heaven in Daniel's day still the same as our God?

For children of other faiths
You will need to show sensitivity when developing the aims of this session. Do not develop the session in such a way that it could be considered you are saying 'my God is better than your god'. Focus rather on Daniel's faith that God would help him and the fact that the king recognised that Daniel's God could do something that no one else could do. Remember that Daniel trusted God to reveal his power and he helped the king who then came to that understanding. If you are asked questions about God, share stories that show how he has answered prayers in your life or done some amazing things, but do not be drawn into making comparisons. Let the Holy Spirit reveal God's greatness.

For children with additional needs
Many children find communication difficult and so pictures and signing are a great way to help understanding. Children with Down's Syndrome are often very pleased to sign. It would be great to let these children demonstrate that, like Daniel, they have special abilities by signing for the memory verse, but be aware that these children have a 'black and white' way of reacting to challenges. There may be loud tears or running away to 'hide' somewhere, maybe under a table. Give the child space for a time, then approach with confidence and humour. Ignore the behaviour if possible using positive 'I' statements to say what you would like to happen, for example, 'I would like you to help us with the signing'.

Lieutenants' briefing
Spiritual preparation

Read together
Daniel 2:1–3,14–19,46, 47 and outline the threads of the Bible story.

Explore together
This is not an easy chapter: the setting is so different from our lives. But the non-Christian world talks about dreams and interpretations: it may be something that team members are familiar with and it's worth spending a few minutes thinking through our own reactions. In Daniel, this is not 'of God' – but it also not ignored or dismissed as 'nonsense'. Consider together what a Christian response should be. How will you answer a child who asks about dreams and visions – or who asks if their dreams will come true?

This was literally a life or death situation for Daniel and his friends. Notice how Daniel mixes action with prayer – it's not one or the other. Encourage the team today to mix action and prayer, and then, at the end when God has answered prayer, be sure to praise him (see verses 20–23).

Run through the aims for the day (those listed on page 39 and others that you have chosen for the club), and think through and chat informally about how these are going to be met through the time together.

Reflect together
Have you ever really prayed to God to prevent something unpleasant from happening? Have you ever really asked God for wisdom beyond normal human wisdom? If you have, what happened? If not, is it because you haven't needed to – or because you're not sure what would happen?

The 'new' kingdom of the dream is interpreted as the kingdom of heaven, which Christians believe starts with Jesus. Pause for a moment before the busy, happy chaos of the club and let that sense of being part of God's kingdom fill, energise and inspire you.

Pray together
Pray for today's session that God would give all the team wisdom so that they can see the children as God sees them, and that they share the Bible message in the way that God wants them to. Pray for each other, for good relationships within the team, for stamina, boldness, patience and to be good examples to the children.

Practical preparation
Talk through your programme together, remind everyone of the programme and who is doing what, ensuring that everyone knows their part in the day and has everything they need. Pay special attention to younger leaders and helpers or those who have not taken part in your holiday club before: give them an extra boost of encouragement.

Set up the different areas of the club and make sure that everything is in place in plenty of time, so you are ready as the first children come from the registration area.

Listen to any last-minute information or instructions from your Fleet admiral.

Encourage the team to greet children who came to the club yesterday and welcome everyone.

Share a 'team booster' before heading into the club. (For example, stand closely in a circle, with one arm out and touching hands with everyone else; say together 'Be bold, be strong, for the Lord our God is with us.')

Remember to smile!

What you need checklist

- **Registration** Registration forms, badges, labels, pens, team lists
- **Starbases** Bibles, *Daniel's Data* or *Star Sheets*, Bible discovery notes
- **Music** The Transporters band or backing tracks
- **Drama** Costumes and props
- **Technology** PA system, laptop, PowerPoints and projection/OHP and acetates, *Space Academy* DVD
- **Activities** Equipment for games and construction
- **The Captain** Running order, notes, Full throttle and One giant leap equipment, quiz questions and props
- **The Space Commander** Story script, flip chart or sketchboard
- **Café Cosmos** Drinks and biscuits or other refreshments

Space programme
As the children arrive and register, play some space-related or sci-fi music (such as *Star Trek*, *Star Wars* or *Dr Who*) and display the *Space Academy* logo on the screen to welcome the children.

Have welcome people ready to greet the children and take them to their groups. Encourage the group leaders to be ready to welcome back those who came yesterday and to expect new children in their groups.

Report to starbase
10 minutes small groups

Welcome the children to the Starbase, especially any new ones. Let these add a star or planet with their name on to the mobile made yesterday. Now do the following activity.

Space vehicles
What you need
- Square of cooking foil for each child

What you do
Give everyone a square of cooking foil and ask them to mould it into some sort of space vehicle. As they are doing this, chat about the fact that on a space journey we would need to be protected. What might we need to be protected from? And in real life can they think of any time they have been protected from danger? If you have a suitable personal story to tell, do so now.

Admire all the models. Make sure everyone's is identifiable in some way so you know who they belong to. Put them in a container ready for easy collection later on.

VOYAGE 2 **THE DIFFICULT DREAM**

Action stations

45 minutes
all together

Play the *Space Academy* song as a sign that the Starbases should come together as a big group. The Captain should welcome the children to *Space Academy*, especially any newcomers. See if they can remember what yesterday's story was about.

Phaser-fitness

Super Nova should lead a workout, reminding the astronauts of the need to be fit to carry out their space voyage! Use the simple exercises you used in the first session, adding in one or two more. Begin today with everyone asleep and slowly get them to wake up, stretching one limb after another. Build up to a more vigorous aerobic routine.

Brain boosters

The Captain introduces Buzz Brain who's yawning and looking tired. The Captain asks him what's wrong and Buzz relates some strange dream he had that involved climbing a mountain. The Captain reminds the children to listen out for a dream and a mountain in today's story. 'But first, what brain booster are you going to share with us today, Buzz?'

Buzz then shares the following facts:

1 How do astronauts sleep in space? There isn't enough room on board a space shuttle for beds so they have small compartments or sleeping bags. The biggest difference is that there's no gravity in space, so there isn't really an up or a down. Sometimes astronauts sleep standing up. Their sleeping bag is strapped to the walls so they don't float around and bump themselves in their sleep!

2 There is a very large mountain that I can guarantee none of you have been to. It's found on the planet Mars. It's called Olympus Mons and is 27 km (or 27,000 metres) high. That's almost three times bigger than Earth's Mount Everest which is 8,848 metres above sea level!

Full throttle

Moon dust

What you need

- Two mounds of flour (press flour into a bowl and turn it out onto a plate)
- Six sweets (such as vegetarian wine gums or midget gems)
- Two rounded plastic knives
- Cover-up and clean-up equipment

What you do

Ask for two volunteers (leaders or children) and give each of them a mound of flour with three sweets placed on top. Tell the volunteers that they have to slice some of the flour away without causing the sweets to fall off. If a sweet falls, then they have to retrieve it with their mouth. Declare the person who dislodges the fewest sweets the winner! (If you are feeling particularly mean, you could spray the volunteers' faces with water before they stick them in the flour!)

Star songs

Get The Transporters to remind the children of the *Space Academy* theme song and sing it again. Add other songs, mostly repeating those from yesterday, but perhaps introducing one new one. If some children already know a song, get them to come out and help teach it to the others, especially if it has actions or dance movements.

One giant leap

This activity ties into the passage as it introduces the idea of trying to work out what something is.

Quarantine

What you need

- several items that have a distinctive 'feel' (such as a hairbrush, a bar of soap, an apple, a book)
- blindfolds or bags

What you do

Ask for volunteers and bring them to the front. Blindfold each one and then give them one of the objects you have collected. Each volunteer should try to guess what the item is by feel alone. The winner is the one who guesses the most.

Tell the story

For each Voyage, there are three options suggested for telling the Bible story: you can use the same approach each time, mix and match how you tell the story, or combine two or more approaches. Choose which will be most helpful for your team, your children and the style of your club.

1 The Space Commander now goes on to tell the Bible story based on Daniel 2:1–6,12–19,31–49 using their own words if possible (see page 7 for tips on how to do this). You can use the section headings, keywords and visual ideas from the script (see option 3) as memory joggers and to vary your story presentation each time.

2 Introduce today's episode from the *Space Academy* DVD. (If you are telling the story and using the DVD, tell the story first, then show the DVD so the children already have the outline of the events before seeing the episode.)

3 Or the Space Commander may prefer to follow the fully scripted retold Bible story for Voyage 2 on page 73.

Using visuals

Today's script has prompts for including visuals. You can do this in a number of ways: draw the different elements on a flip chart or a large sheet of paper as you go, use a 'sketchboard' with paints. (The bigger you can make this the better: a large-scale visual aid will reinforce what you're saying about the enormous statue.) If you prefer, you could encourage someone creative in your team to do this part while you tell the story, although it is very straightforward, as follows:

1 A crown with a part of a circle underneath to form the king's head for each of the four sections. When it gets to the relevant section, you fill in the eyes and mouth to show the four feelings: worried, angry, surprised and happy.

2 Keywords dream, kill, statue and future which can just be written in, or you can do them in 'lightning lettering', where you start with a box for each letter and fill in the bits to make the letter appear.

CAPTAIN'S LOG 4

3 A drawing of the statue for Part 3. This can be drawn as really simple blocks: a yellow circle for the gold head, a grey square for the body, an orange or brown square for the waist and black or grey rectangles for the legs. Alternatively, do a bit of junk modelling using different sized boxes.

Universe challenge

Before the session, put together some questions based on the space and astronaut facts the children heard earlier and the Bible passage for the day. You could include:
- What planet is the largest mountain found on?
- When would an astronaut want to be tied up in space? Why?
- At the beginning of today's story, why was the king disturbed?
- What was the dream about?

For today's scoring system, have a small bowl of 'cosmic dust', either of shredded coloured paper or glittery shapes you can buy from any craft supplier. Bury six stars in the 'dust', each one with a number on, from one to six. If a child answers correctly, get them to come up and dip their hand in the cosmic dust and draw out a star to find out their score.

Data check

Using the points below, spend a few moments summing up the teaching for the day.
- Daniel and his friends found themselves facing death through no fault of their own!
- The king had threatened to kill all his advisers if they couldn't tell him the disturbing dream he'd had and its meaning.
- Daniel and his friends turned to God in prayer and God answered by giving Daniel the secret of the dream.
- Daniel, Shadrach, Meshach and Abednego discovered that once again, as they put their trust in God, he helped them.
- God also protected them – being able to give the king the mystery of the dream saved their lives and the lives of others!
- When we face challenges we, too, can turn to God in prayer and God will help and protect us.
- The king didn't know God but he saw that God had power and that God is 'above all other gods and kings'. This was because he could see that no one else was clever enough to interpret his dream – only God could do this.
- When we trust God and do things for him, often, but not always, those around us can see how great God is too.
- God had a purpose for Daniel and his friends in Babylon so once again they were given more responsibility. God has a plan for each of us too.

Prayer

To conclude Action Stations! you may want to pause here to give the children an opportunity to think about what they've learnt and to pray silently. Before the session, create a 'space' prayer action that you can do just before you pray. You could say something like, 'Start to think about what God is like from what you've heard in this story – what would you want to say to him, right now? Because you can do that right now!' Make this time short as the children will probably only be quiet for a minute or so. Say 'Amen' or have another action so everyone knows it is the end of the prayer.

Lunar landing

45 minutes small groups

During this time, remind the leaders to collect any questions for On the star spot and get them to the person being interviewed in plenty of time.

Cafe Cosmos

In your Starbase group have your refreshments together and chat about the club so far. What are the children's favourite parts? Remind your group to think of questions to ask at On the star spot later. Remind them also of the space capsule, where they can leave their jokes and pictures. Go on to explore the Bible passage together more closely.

Bible discovery

This story in the Bible is quite long and complicated so spend a few minutes making sure everyone has an idea of the basic story. Focus on the main storyline and try to avoid getting bogged down in the fine details.

With older children (8–10s)

Read Daniel 2:1–6 on page 13 of *Daniel's Data* and ask the children to attempt to circle the words that describe the dream. (They will soon realise they can't!) Remind them that the king's advisers couldn't describe the dream either. Look together at verse 5 to see what the king says he will do with them as a result. Get the children to imagine what it would be like to be punished for something they haven't done wrong. Encourage them to fill in the face, draw the thought bubbles and fill them in on page 14.

Now read Daniel 2:10–19 on page 15, getting the children to circle the people Daniel spoke to and underlining what he said. Ask how Daniel knew the dream and its meaning. Talk about how you would have felt if you'd been Daniel, once God spoke to him.

Invite the children to fill in the crossword on page 16 and then find out what the dream means by reading Daniel 2:37–39a,44,45 on page 17. Draw the king's face at different times in the story on page 18. Talk about how Daniel had to do something impossible or he and his friends would be killed! He promised to tell the king about the dream even before he knew what it was. He must have really trusted that God would help him.

Talk with the children about the things that really worry them or make them afraid. Are there things that seem impossible? Reassure the children that God will help them with these things and they can trust him, just like Daniel did. Talk about the new kingdom that would never end, mentioned in verse 44. Say how as Christians, we believe this kingdom began when Jesus came to earth. Use this as an opportunity to share what Jesus means to you and the difference he makes in your life.

If appropriate, spend some time in prayer together, thanking God that he helped Daniel to be brave and go to the king, praising God that he told Daniel the dream in the night and asking God to help you with the things that seem impossible to you.

VOYAGE 2 **THE DIFFICULT DREAM**

With younger children (5-7s)
Look at the two pictures on *Star Sheet 2* and encourage the children to find ten differences between them. Remind the children that the king had a dream and was so cross he was going to kill his advisors if they couldn't tell him the dream and its meaning. Go on to read Daniel 2:12–19, 36–39a,44,45 using a child-friendly Bible or retell the story in your own words.

Look at the words that describe God and talk about how we know he is these things. Fit the words into the rocket grid.

Talk about what they think Daniel discovered about God then follow the line to read about one thing he discovered: 'God helps and protects his friends'.

If you have an appropriate story about how God helped and protected you, tell the children about it now. Encourage the children to think about what they want to say to God in response to today's story. If appropriate, pray together.

With all ages
Adapt these questions to suit your group, sharing your own feelings, opinions and experiences as appropriate:
- Why did the king want his advisers to tell him the dream and the meaning?
- Why couldn't they do it?
- What do you think about the king's demand?
- How do you think Daniel felt when he went to the king to ask him for more time?
- Why could Daniel give the king his answer?
- Who helped Daniel? (God and also his friends; Daniel asked them to pray too: we can always do that. We are not alone. God gives us friends and a whole Christian family to pray with us and for us.)
- Is there anything that really worries you, makes you afraid or seems impossible?
- Do you think God can help you with this?

Shuttlecraft
Choose a construction activity from page 68. For extra craft ideas, see *Ultimate Craft* (SU, 978 1 84427 364 5).

Fit for space
Check that your astronauts are fit for space by choosing a games activity from page 70. For extra games ideas, see *Ultimate Games* (SU, 978 1 84427 365 2).

Red alert!
25 minutes all together

Space capsule
Welcome everyone back together by playing the *Space Academy* theme song. Read out some of the messages and pictures from the space capsule. Thank all the contributing astronauts and remind everyone to bring in more jokes and pictures tomorrow.

Star songs
The Transporters lead the children in a couple of lively songs.

Data recall
The Captain rounds up what the Starbases have been exploring together, recapping the following points:
- Daniel and his friends faced death but were saved because God told Daniel the meaning of the king's dream.
- The king realised that Daniel's God was greatest of all.
- As a result the king gave Daniel and his friends even more responsibility.
- We can trust God to help and protect us.

Cosmic code
Recap Proverbs 3 verse 5. Today, use a rap to teach the verse. Write or print two or three of the words onto large sheets of card, that some children can hold up in the right order. Everyone else can click their fingers or clap two fingers against their palm, and say the words in time to the rhythm; the bold words show the beat. Trust in the Lord with all your heart. Never rely on what you think you know. Proverbs 3 verse 5 – ahahh, ahahh, ahahh. The last bit is not in the Bible but makes the rap go better (you can even tell the children that). A child in the audience chooses a card to be taken away, the child holding it goes to sit down, and you say the verse again. Repeat the process until there are no cards left and see who can do it on their own.

(Go to www.scriptureunion.org.uk/spaceacademy for ideas on using a different verse each day.)

On the star spot
Make a significant feature of this time to talk about Jesus and the possibility of relationship with him. Interview one of the Lieutenants or Ensigns about a time when they have had to rely on God. What event in Jesus' life helps them to learn from Jesus' reliance on God?

Be direct! You do not need to go into the details of the problem but ask the interviewee about times when life or decisions were tough or difficult: how did it make a difference to have Jesus as a friend?

Also include the question you have picked out from those the children thought of; invite them to come up and ask it and give them their 'prize'. When you have finished, thank the Lieutenant or Ensign for being On the star spot!

Drama: The final frontier
Introduce the next episode of the comedy-drama, 'The final frontier'. Today the crew land on a mysterious planet with an unpronounceable name and with jelly-like life forms. Will the crew be successful in their mission to spread the good news of goodness, kindness, generosity, honesty and mercy? Let's find out.

Final orbit
Round off Red alert! by asking the children what they have enjoyed at *Space Academy* today and then include those things in a short prayer of thanks, using your space prayer action. Encourage the children to come back tomorrow by saying something similar to the following:

'Well it's been an action-packed day but there's more to come. What other test of courage, faith and being different will Daniel, Shadrach, Meshach and Abednego have to face? Will the evil Odor overpower the crew of the Starship (Name) with his evil odour? Will Buzz Brain's dreams frazzle his brain or will he have more brain boosters for you? What cracking jokes will the Captain

CAPTAIN'S LOG 4

find in the space capsule? Join us on Voyage 3 tomorrow to find out!'

Sing the *Space Academy* theme song and send the astronauts back to their Starbases to round off the day's session.

Touchdown

10 minutes
small groups

Creative prayer

Remember together how Daniel trusted God. It was especially important in today's story, but Daniel trusted God all the time. He prayed when things were tough – but he was carrying on as he always did, praying every day, several times a day.

Get out the container with the foil models your group made earlier. Ask the children to take turns to take a model out that's not their own and say, 'I pray that the person who made this will trust God' and then see if they can give it to the right owner. This person then has their turn at picking out a model.

Voyage clear-up

30 minutes
team time

After all the children have gone, clear up from the day's events and set up for the next session, if the premises you are using makes that feasible. Meet together as a team to debrief. Use a feedback system that works best for you – there is an evaluation form on the *Space Academy* website. This would be the time for the Fleet admiral to raise any obvious issues. Also raise anything that has cropped up that needs sorting before tomorrow and assign someone to sort it out. Remember to praise the team for the things that went well and urge them to do as well or better tomorrow! Have a brief time of prayer where Lieutenants and Ensigns can pray for their groups, and other team members can pray for their areas of responsibility. If you have the time and the facilities, you may wish to share a meal together.

PHOTOCOPIABLE PAGE

VOYAGE 2 **THE DIFFICULT DREAM**

Star sheet Voyage 2
The difficult dream

Bible fun with a friend or on your own.

1 Can you find ten differences between these two pictures of the king's dream?

2 God is… Can you fit the words that describe God into the grid on the rocket?

- powerful
- strong
- living
- perfect
- wise

TRAINEE'S LOG 2

3 Follow along the line to see what Daniel discovered about God.

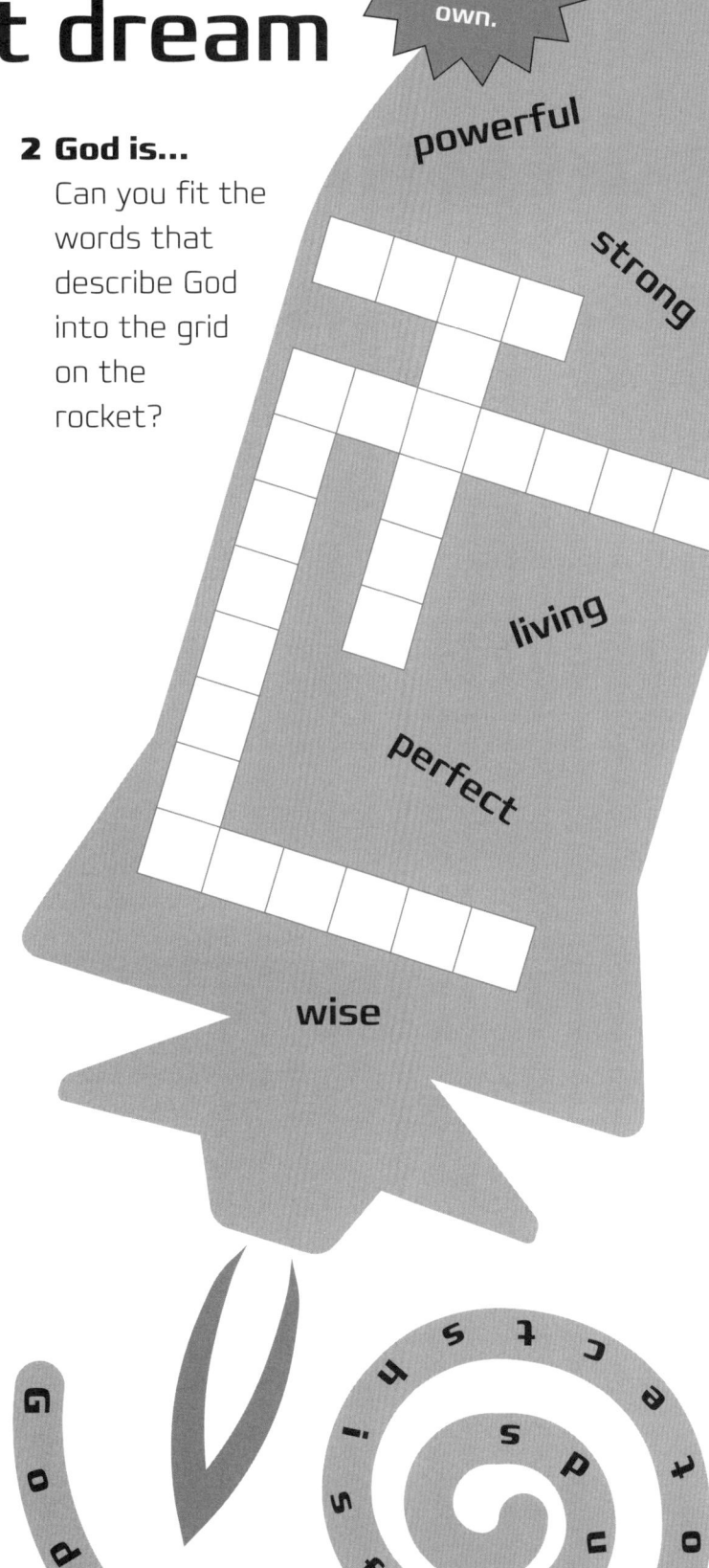

God helps and protects his friends

45

SPACE ACADEMY

Voyage 3
Stunning statue

Key passage
Daniel 3

Key storylines
- Shadrach, Meshach and Abednego risk their lives by refusing to bow and worship a statue.
- King Nebuchadnezzar threatens them with being burned in a flaming furnace but they still refuse.
- They are thrown into the fire but are not harmed – and a fourth person is seen in the fire with them.
- They come out of the furnace and the king acknowledges the power of God and promotes them, again.

Key aims
- To show that Shadrach, Meshach and Abednego stood firm for what they believed and God honoured their faith.
- To demonstrate God's awesome power and discover that worshipping God is the most important thing in the world.
- To continue to build relationships with the children and welcome those who are new to the club today.

Further aim
- To explore the meaning of the story further, in the light of what we know about Jesus.

For children with no church background
Much in today's culture encourages 'worship' of celebrity, fame and stardom, and many children, bombarded with images of pop, TV and sports stars, will want to be like them. The idea of only bowing down to the God of heaven will indeed be alien to some. In a country where religious freedom is allowed, it may also seem strange that people could be killed for putting God first.

For church children
Church children might have heard this story before, but are most likely to remember the facts of the incredible escape from the furnace rather than the reason why the three men were thrown in there. Help them to think about times when they might be put under pressure to conform, and how Jesus could help them still to put God first. Standing up for God to the extent of being killed for it is a very adult concept, so be sure you deal with it appropriately for the age of the children.

For children of other faiths
Today's subject of being different and worshipping a different god would be a familiar one for those from other faith backgrounds. You may want to emphasise that the three friends had to consider what they were going to do and then decided to follow God whatever the consequences. They were willing to stand by their decision even though it meant punishment. Please consider the principles of working with those from other faith backgrounds as you prepare for this session. How would you respond if a child wanted to follow Jesus? What would you say to them?

For children with additional needs
Worshipping God can be done in many ways. Children without voices are able to worship using streamers and instruments, but be aware that children on the autistic spectrum may well like to borrow ear defenders if it all gets very loud. Sometimes just wearing them around the neck is enough to help a child feel safe. Big, cheap ear defenders are available from tools merchants. Phaser-fitness could be finger exercises or even eye movements for those with physical limitations.

VOYAGE 3 **STUNNING STATUE**

Lieutenants' briefing

Spiritual preparation

Read together
Read Daniel 3:8–18.

Think together
Lots of people believe in other gods today, as did King Neb. The Bible is clear that there is only one true, living God, the God of heaven. How can this story help us relate to those who believe in other gods, maybe including some of the children who will come today?

Reflect together
Shadrach, Meshach and Abednego had a tremendous commitment to God. Being on the team for *Space Academy* shows our commitment and may mean explaining to our friends why, but it is unlikely that we will have to stand up for God in the way that these three did. What difference would it make to us if we were in their position?

Spend a few moments looking again at verses 16–18: be inspired by the faith and trust of these three men. Think back to Voyage 1 when they made a relatively small stand for God and see how that prepared them for this much greater test. As you read the story, you know the outcome – but of course, they did not. That is an awesome thought.

Pray together
Pray that God will make himself obvious to all those who come to *Space Academy* today, whether it's team, children, parents bringing and collecting children, or visitors. Pray that everyone will know that the God of heaven is real and just as powerful today as he was all those years ago. Pray for each other, for good relationships within the team, for stamina, boldness, patience and to be good examples to the children.

Practical preparation
Talk through your programme together, remind everyone of the programme and who is doing what, ensuring that everyone knows their part in the day and has everything they need. Pay special attention to younger leaders and helpers or those who have not taken part in your holiday club before: give them an extra boost of encouragement.

Set up the different areas of the club and make sure that everything is in place in plenty of time, so you are ready as the first children come from the registration area.

Listen to any last-minute information or instructions from your Fleet admiral. It would be good if today they could give the team an extra pep talk as teams may flag a bit midweek.

Encourage the team to greet and welcome everyone.

Share a 'team booster' before heading into the club. (For example, stand closely in a circle, with one arm out and touching hands with everyone else; say together 'Be bold, be strong, for the Lord our God is with us.')

Remember to smile!

What you need checklist

- **Registration** Registration forms, badges, labels, pens, team lists
- **Starbases** Bibles, *Daniel's Data* or *Star Sheets*, Bible discovery notes
- **Music** The Transporters band or backing tracks
- **Drama** Costumes and props
- **Technology** PA system, laptop, PowerPoints and projection/OHP and acetates, *Space Academy* DVD
- **Activities** Equipment for games and construction
- **The Captain** Running order, notes, Full throttle and One giant leap equipment, quiz questions and props
- **The Space Commander** Story script and musical instruments
- **Café Cosmos** Drinks and biscuits or other refreshments

Space programme
As the children arrive and register, play some space-related or sci-fi music (such as *Star Trek*, *Star Wars* or *Dr Who*) and display the *Space Academy* logo on the screen to welcome the children.

Have a welcome team on hand to take the children to their groups. Encourage the group leaders to be ready to welcome the children in their groups, especially any new ones.

Report to starbase
10 minutes **small groups**

Strange planet
What you need
- Plastic ball (ball pond ball)

What you do
After welcoming the children, and especially any newcomers, ask them to think of the strangest place they have been to. This could be somewhere they went on holiday or an unusual shop, theme park or perhaps a show. Produce a plastic ball saying, 'This is our strange planet' and write the unusual places on it as the children tell you them. If you wish, think up a name for your planet. You could tell them that Daniel's friends also go to a very strange place today – not a planet, but certainly nowhere we have ever been.

Action Stations
45 minutes **all together**

Play the *Space Academy* theme song as a sign for the children to join the larger group. The Captain should welcome everyone to *Space Academy* and briefly run through what's in store today. See if anyone can remember what you've been learning about this week.

Phaser-fitness
Super Nova should lead the workout, using moves from the previous two days. Introduce several bowing down and kneeling actions today. Remember to include actions suitable for children with special needs, if necessary. Everyone needs

CAPTAIN'S LOG 4

SPACE ACADEMY

CAPTAIN'S LOG 4

to be in good shape to be launched on their space adventure!

Brain boosters

The Captain says how in today's story the children will be hearing about some loud music and a very, very hot place. He invites Buzz Brain to come and share his brain boosters once again.

Buzz Brain shares the following facts:

1 Venus is the hottest planet in our solar system. It has temperatures up to 461°C – that's well over twice as hot as your oven at home! Although Venus isn't as close to the sun as Mercury, it gets hotter because it has a thick yellow cloud above in the atmosphere. This acts like a greenhouse and it traps the heat so there is nowhere for it to escape to.

2 Mission Control (that's the men back on Earth who are in contact with the astronauts) traditionally send wake-up music to astronauts each morning when they're on the space shuttle. The astronauts' families or Mission Control select the songs. Sometimes they have a theme related to what's happening on the shuttle

Full throttle

Asteroid field

What you need
- Shaving foam
- Cheese puff snacks (such as Wotsits)
- Shower caps (optional)
- Cover-up and clean-up equipment

What you do
Ask for four volunteers, and put them into two pairs. Put shaving foam on the face of one of the pair, and give the cheesy puffs to the other. (If you're concerned about allergies, give one volunteer a shower cap and put the shaving foam on that.) At a given signal, the players with the cheesy puffs have to throw them at their partner, who should try to catch them in the shaving foam. At the end of a time limit (or when they have no cheesy puffs left), count the number caught in the foam. The pair with the most is the winner.

Star Songs

Reintroduce The Transporters and use mostly songs that you have already done with the children, perhaps including another new one, especially if some of the children could help the others to learn it.

You could finish with the *Space Academy* theme song, and include any actions you might have come up with!

One giant leap

This activity ties into the Bible passage as it is based around building a statue.

Spaceman statues

What you need
- Five boxes per group
- Paint

What you do
Before the session, pile each set of five boxes on top of each other, and paint a picture of a spaceman or robot down one side (so that, when you take the pile down, you end up with five sections of the spaceman/robot). Colour code your pictures. Hide the boxes around your venue.

Ask for two or three volunteers from each group to come to the front. Explain that each group has a space statue that they need to reconstruct, and that all the pieces of their statue are hidden around the room/venue. Give each group a colour and send the volunteers off to find that colour spaceman/robot. The other group members should encourage their volunteers. As they find the pieces, they should pile them up at the front. The first to reconstruct their statue is the winner.

Tell the story

For each Voyage, there are three options suggested for telling the Bible story: you can use the same approach each time, mix and match how you tell the story, or combine two or more approaches. Choose which will be most helpful for your team, your children and the style of your club.

1 The Space Commander now goes on to tell the Bible story based on Daniel 3 using their own words if possible (see page 7 for tips on how to do this). You can use the section headings and interactive ideas from the script (see option 3) as memory joggers and to vary your story presentation each time.

2 Introduce today's episode from the *Space Academy* DVD. (If you are telling the story and using the DVD, tell the story first, then show the DVD so the children already have the outline of the events before seeing the episode.)

3 Or the Space Commander may prefer to follow the fully scripted retold Bible story for Voyage 3 on page 74.

Involving the children

This story is great for involving the children, especially those who know something about it already, although it's obviously not a good idea to encourage the children to act out bowing down to the statue! You could collect as many musical instruments as you can find, and be brave enough to invite volunteers to come out and play them at the appropriate time in the story. It'll probably be a terrible racket, but lots of fun. Alternatively, you could divide the children up into different sections, telling each to pretend to play an instrument when you conduct them. The Bible says there were 'flutes, trumpets, harps – and all other kinds of musical instruments', so you can really have whatever you like! It may work best to give the children a tune that you want them to pretend to play; perhaps 'We are the champions' or 'We will rock you' by Queen or something that relates to the king thinking that his god is the greatest. Whatever you choose to do, make sure you have a signal, such as a 'thumbs up' sign, to show the children when to start playing and a signal, such as a 'cut' sign, to show when they need to stop, so that it doesn't descend into chaos!

You can also involve the children in the furnace part of the story, by letting them be the flames. Practise beforehand: for small flames, weave your hands in and out of each other and upwards. For when the furnace gets really hot, act out large flames using the whole body, twisting up and up from sitting to standing.

Universe challenge

Before the session, put together some questions based on the space and astronaut facts the children heard earlier and the Bible passage for the day. You could include:
- Which is the hottest planet?
- What kind of alarm clock do astronauts have?
- What was the king's statue made of?
- What would happen to anyone who didn't bow down and worship the king's statue?

For today's scoring system, have six glow-in-the-dark small hoops or necklaces and a free-standing kitchen roll holder or similar upright 'pole'. If a child answers a question correctly, get them to come up and try to throw as many rings as they can over the pole. The number of rings is the number of points they score.

Data check

Using the points below, spend a few moments summing up the teaching for the day.
- Shadrach, Meshach and Abednego faced death once again – this time because they stood up for their faith by refusing to bow and worship a statue.
- The king threatened Shadrach, Meshach and Abednego with being burned in a flaming furnace if they didn't bow down, but they still refused.
- Their reason was amazing. They believed God could save them – but even if he didn't they still would not worship others!
- Lots of things in the world around us today can distract us from worshipping God alone. There is often pressure to do things that others do and to follow the crowd – even when we know it's something God doesn't want us to do. The easy thing is to do what everyone else is doing. But worshipping God is the most important thing in the world.
- When the three friends did what God wanted, he sent someone special to be with them in the furnace. Who could it have been? When you get to your Starbases in a short while, look closely at Daniel 3:25 and talk about who you think it was. Whoever it was, the three friends were saved and the flaming furnace didn't harm them! Today, we have someone special to be with us in whatever our circumstances. That person is Jesus.

Prayer

To conclude Action Stations! you may want to pause here to give the children an opportunity to think about what they've learnt and to pray silently. Before the session, create a 'space' prayer action that you can do just before you pray. You could say something like, 'Start to think about what God is like from what you've heard in this story – what would you want to say to him, right now? Because you can do that right now!' Make this time short as the children will probably only be quiet for a minute or so. Say 'Amen' or have another action so everyone knows it is the end of the prayer.

Lunar landing

45 minutes small groups

During this time, remind the leaders to collect any questions for On the star spot and get them to the person being interviewed in plenty of time.

Cafe Cosmos

Serve your chosen refreshments together and chat about the club so far. What are the children's favourite parts? Remind the Starbases to think of questions to ask at On the star spot later. Remind them also of the space capsule, where they can leave their jokes and pictures. Go on to explore the Bible passage together more closely.

Bible discovery

With older children (8-10s)

Together, work out the measurements on page 20 of *Daniel's Data*. (Include the suggestion of lying on the floor in a circle.) Read Daniel 3:1–7 from page 21 and get the children to underline the words of the king's command and circle the words that say what would happen if anyone disobeyed. Chat about what you would have done if you'd been there. Now read Daniel 3:16–21 on page 22 and get the children to crack the code on page 23. Talk about how amazing it was that these men trusted God that much. Let the children draw the flames on page 24 and fill in the names of people who need prayer in each flame. Ask them what they want to say to God about the people on their flames. Read the last part of the story, Daniel 3:24–28, on page 25 and get the children to draw a circle around the words that they think are most 'Wow!' and chat with them about anything that doesn't make sense to them.

Talk about the fact that it wasn't easy or safe living God's way in Babylon! Shadrach, Meshach and Abednego were threatened with a horrible death if they stood firm for God and chose to worship only him. Ask the children to write three words on page 26 to describe what they think these men are like. Talk about what God is like in this story, the things they thought God would do and the things he actually did.

When the three friends did what God wanted, he sent someone special to be with them in the furnace. Look closely at Daniel 3:25 together and talk about who they think it was. (It could have been Jesus/God/an angel). Spend a short while praising God for his power.

With younger children (5-7s)

Read Daniel 3 using a child-friendly Bible or retell it with your own words. Ask the children to think of words they'd use to describe Shadrach, Meshach and Abednego.

Look at the picture on *Star Sheet 3* and encourage the children to join the dots to see the fourth person in the fire. Talk together about who this might be. Answers could include Jesus, an angel, God. Say that we can't be sure but he was 'of God' and he rescued them. Get the children to fill in the missing vowels (you may need to explain what vowels are) in the words. Ask the children to think of things that show that God is powerful, wonderful, amazing – eg, things in creation, that he answers prayer, that he loves us, etc. Get the children to draw a line from the phrases in the stars to the words 'yes' or 'no'. Go on to talk about the differences between those things

CAPTAIN'S LOG 4

that show we worship God and those things that don't. End with a prayer praising God for his power and asking him to help us worship him.

With all ages
Note: the Bible does not mention Daniel in this story. As a governor, he may have been in another part of the country. From what else we know about him, he would not have been one of the crowd who did decide to bow to the statue.

Adapt these questions to suit your group, sharing your own feelings, opinions and experiences as appropriate:
- Has anyone seen a statue in a museum or art gallery? What was it like? What was it made of?
- What would you have done at the dedication of the statue? Bowed to the statue or not?
- What words would you use to describe Shadrach, Meshach and Abednego in this story?
- Think back to the story in Voyage 1 and how these friends took the relatively small decision not to eat the king's food? How might that small 'stand' have prepared them for this much more dangerous choice?
- What is God like in this story?
- How can we find the courage we need to remain faithful to God during times of trouble, pressure or persecution? (And what might trouble, pressure and persecution look like in our lives? It's not very likely to be a flaming furnace – but what could it be?)
- This story shows that worshipping God is important. Have you 'worshipped' him during *Space Academy*? How?

Shuttlecraft
Choose a construction activity from page 69. For extra craft ideas, see *Ultimate Craft* (SU, 978 1 84427 364 5).

Fit for space
Check that your astronauts are fit for space by choosing a games activity from page 70. For extra games ideas, see *Ultimate Games* (SU, 978 1 84427 365 2).

Red alert!
25 minutes all together

Space capsule
Welcome everyone back together by playing the *Space Academy* theme song. Read out some of the messages and pictures from the space capsule. Thank all the contributing astronauts and remind everyone to bring in more jokes and pictures tomorrow.

Star songs
The Transporters lead the children in a couple of lively songs.

Data recall
The Captain rounds up what the Starbases have been exploring together, recapping the following points:
- Shadrach, Meshach and Abednego risked their lives by refusing to bow and worship a statue and were thrown into a flaming furnace.
- They were not harmed – and a fourth person was seen in the fire with them – God saved them.
- They came out of the furnace and the king acknowledged the power of God; the king promoted them, again.
- Worshipping God is the most important thing in the world.
- When we stand firm in what we believe, God is pleased about it.
- Today, we can choose to live God's way and be friends of Jesus.

Cosmic code
Today, teach the children the second part of the Learn and remember verse: verse 6. In advance, write the words on seven card stars divided as follows: Remember the Lord/ in everything/ you do,/ and he will/ show you/ the right way./ Proverbs 3:6. String up a washing line and have some volunteers come up and peg the stars to the line in the right order. Learn the verse together and as you get more confident let some stars fall to the ground (shooting stars!).

On the star spot
This is a key opportunity to demonstrate that being a follower of Jesus may be testing. Team members have been showing the children, day by day, what it's like to be a follower of Jesus. Today, however, look for an example that is extraordinary and will startle the children, not because it is dangerous but because Jesus made a tangible difference.

Interview one of the Lieutenants or Ensign about a time when they had to do something brave rather than let God down. Ask, too, about the words that Jesus said to his disciples – 'I am with you always' – and how knowing that Jesus is with them gives them the ability and confidence to be brave.

Also include the question you have picked out from those the children thought of; invite them to ask their question and give them their 'prize'. When you have finished, thank the Lieutenant or Ensign for being On the star spot!

Drama: The final frontier
Introduce the next episode of the comedy-drama, 'The final frontier'. Once again the crew attempt to spread the good news of Mission Command, with goodness, kindness, generosity, honesty and mercy, this time on the planet of 'Ware ah ya'. But will they accomplish what they set out to achieve or will the evil Odor overpower them with his evil smell?

Final orbit
Round off Red alert! by asking the children what they have enjoyed at *Space Academy* today and then include those things in a short prayer of thanks, using your space prayer action.

Encourage the children to come back tomorrow by saying something similar to the following:

'It's been a very exciting trip, today! But the adventure is not over. What other strange goings-on will there be in Babylon for Daniel, Shadrach, Meshach and Abednego in the Bible story? Will Buzz's brain have been frazzled by the extreme heat of Planet Venus? Will Prism have recovered from his marshmallow-induced stupor? Will you astronauts be fit for space? Come back ready to join *Space Academy* tomorrow!'

Sing the *Space Academy* theme song and send the astronauts back to their Starbases to round off the day's session.

Touchdown

10 minutes
small groups

Creative prayer

Show the strange planet ball you made together earlier. Remind the children of the unusual places they have been to and that wherever they were, God was with them. Talk about why Daniel's friends went into the fire: they knew worshipping God was the most important thing, and they found that God is all powerful.

Toss the ball to each other. The person throwing says, 'Let's worship God', and the one catching (or everyone) replies, 'He is great and powerful.' Try to make sure everyone has a turn.

Voyage clear-up

30 minutes
team time

After all the children have gone, clear up from the day's events and set up for the next session, if the premises you are using makes that feasible. Meet together as a team to debrief. Use a feedback system that works best for you – there is an evaluation form on the *Space Academy* website. This would be the time for the Fleet admiral to raise any obvious issues. Also raise anything that has cropped up that needs sorting before tomorrow and assign someone to sort it out. Remember to praise the team for the things that went well and urge them to do as well or better tomorrow! Have a brief time of prayer where Lieutenants and Ensigns can pray for their groups, and other team members can pray for their areas of responsibility. If you have the time and the facilities, you may wish to share a meal together.

Star sheet Voyage 3
Stunning statue

Bible fun with a friend or on your own.

1 Join the dots to see the fourth person in the fire.

2 Fill in the missing letters.
Daniel's friends worshipped God because he is…

a	☀
e	★
i	☆
o	○
u	✪

p o w e r f u l

w o n d e r f u l

a m a z i n g

listen to God

NO

3 Join the phrases in the star shapes to the YES or NO planets to show the ways we can worship God.

- obey our parents
- tell lies
- try our best
- thank God
- steal
- pray
- kick people
- play fairly

YES

Voyage 4
The heavenly hand

Key passage
Daniel 5

Key storylines
- King Belshazzar mocks God by using treasures from the Temple for his own banquet.
- A hand appears and writes a message on the wall: the king is terrified and no one at the banquet knows what the words mean.
- Daniel explains the message – and it comes true that night when the country is taken over by another powerful nation and Darius becomes king.

Key aims
- To hear how Belshazzar found out that God is real and powerful and how it matters how people treat him.
- To be challenged about our own attitudes to, and relationship with, God.
- To continue to build relationships with the children and be ready to discuss things with them that arise from the stories and activities in *Space Academy*.

For children with no church background
In an age where children's fiction includes popular series of stories about people who can do magic or have supernatural powers, it is helpful to stress that it was God, not Daniel, who made the writing appear, and he could do that because he is so powerful – greater than any other power.

For church children
You may want to ask older children with a church background if they can think of ways that people in church don't always treat God as he deserves: perhaps taking him for granted, or ignoring him. Help them to grasp that because of Jesus' death on the cross, God will not punish people as he did Belshazzar, but will forgive those who trust in him.

For children of other faiths
As the week goes on, take opportunities to talk to the families of the children who come. Ask them if their children are enjoying the club and if they are happy with everything. This will reassure parents that you are not trying to undermine them. The theme of God being part of everyday life and prayer might be familiar with children of different faiths. In Hinduism and Sikhism behaviour is more important than beliefs, and following the example of Mohammed is a central part of Islam. The children might be able to share how their faith affects their behaviour which could lead to a good discussion about the ways we step out in faith to follow Jesus.

For children with additional needs
Children might hold challenging attitudes to God if they feel that it is somehow God's doing that they are 'stuck' with a disability. Be ready to listen and thoughtful about what might be provoking difficult behaviour. Challenging behaviour can also occur if a child feels threatened, and there are many ways to remove perceived threats yet help the child understand there are consequences, see *Mega Top Tips on Dealing with challenging behaviour* (Scripture Union 978 1 84427 531).

Lieutenants' briefing

Spiritual preparation

Read together
Give a little background to the story so far before reading Daniel 5:22–31.

Explore together
Daniel wasn't at the party but got called in later. Being available at the right time, in the right place and having the right things to say was significant and, for Daniel, was what mattered, rather than the fame and fortune that the king offered him.

No one – not even a great king – is beyond the reach of God and his Word. God is real, powerful and not to be messed about. Belshazzar ignored this at his peril. This is not an easy story to tell to children as it is a stark warning. Whilst we want children to trust in God as their friend, we must always remember that God is to be respected and worshipped.

Run through the aims for the day (those listed on page 53 and others that you have chosen for the club), and think through and chat informally about how these are going to be met through the time together.

Reflect together
How well have we learnt the lessons of our past in relation to God? Are there times when we are proud or disobey God? Do our lives show that we worship him above all else? How do we know? This story can challenge us about our own attitudes and behaviour – but we do not need to despair: no one is beyond the reach of God and his Word, in a positive way.

Four days into *Space Academy*, are there people you are finding 'difficult'? In an open club, you may be struggling to build relationships with some of the children: you may find their behaviour testing; they may seem too noisy, too quiet or too demanding. Be inspired by this story to take up the challenge, knowing that God can find a way to speak both to them and you today. (And remember you are part of a team, with Jesus as the leader!)

Pray together
Pray that all we do today may give honour to God and show that we worship him. Ask for his help to explain this story with its serious warning in such a way that children may not be frightened, but be able to respond by putting their trust in him.

Pray about those 'difficult' relationships and situations, asking God to work in the lives of the children – and in and through you today. Pray for each other, for good relationships within the team, for stamina, boldness, patience and to be good examples to the children.

Practical preparation

Talk through your programme together, remind everyone of the programme and who is doing what, ensuring that everyone knows their part in the day and has everything they need.

Set up the different areas of the club and make sure that everything is in place in plenty of time, so you are ready as the first children come from the registration area.

Listen to any last-minute information or instructions from your Fleet admiral.

Encourage the team to greet and welcome everyone.

Share a 'team booster' before heading into the club. (For example, stand closely in a circle, with one arm out and touching hands with everyone else; say together 'Be bold, be strong, for the Lord our God is with us.')

Remember to smile!

What you need checklist

- **Registration** Registration forms, badges, labels, pens, team lists
- **Starbases** Bibles, *Daniel's Data* or *Star Sheets*, Bible discovery notes
- **Music** The Transporters band or backing tracks
- **Drama** Costumes and props
- **Technology** PA system, laptop, PowerPoints and projection/OHP and acetates, *Space Academy* DVD
- **Activities** Equipment for games and construction
- **The Captain** Running order, notes, Full throttle and One giant leap equipment, quiz questions and props
- **The Space Commander** Story script, wax candle, paper and paint
- **Café Cosmos** Drinks and biscuits or other refreshments

Space programme

As the children arrive and register, play some space-related or sci-fi music (such as *Star Trek*, *Star Wars* or *Dr Who*) and display the *Space Academy* logo on the screen to welcome the children.

Have a welcome team on hand to take the children to their groups. Encourage the group leaders to be ready to welcome the children in their groups.

Report to starbase

20 minutes **small groups**

Unique identity

What you need
- One sheet of A4 card and one smaller piece of card per person
- Ink pad

What you do
After welcoming the children ask them to look at their hands carefully. Ask them to press a finger on to an ink pad and make one fingerprint on a shared A4 card and one on a smaller separate card. Write names on the back of the small cards then collect them up. Spread them out and see if you can all identify which print matches which on the large card without checking the names.

Talk about how God has made each one of us completely unique and he knows us well. Coming to *Space Academy* is a chance for us to get to know him better.

Action stations

45 minutes **all together**

Play the *Space Academy* theme song as a sign for the children to join the larger group.

The Captain should welcome everyone to *Space Academy* and explain something of what the children can expect today. Remind the astronauts about the space capsule, where they can leave jokes, pictures and questions. Recap what you have been learning about this week.

Phaser-fitness

Super Nova should lead the workout, using moves from the previous two days. Invite some volunteers to come and help lead the workout. Introduce lots of vigorous 'writing in the air' actions as extras today. Everyone needs to get into shape for the astronaut training programme!

Brain boosters

The Captain says how in today's story the children will be hearing a very strange message. He invites Buzz Brain to come up and asks 'What's your theory on the meaning of the message, Buzz?'

Buzz says he thinks it's very straightforward really – nursery school for the likes of him! But he doesn't want to boost the astronauts' brains too much so instead he says he'll share three space facts to go with each part of the message:

- **Number**: Jupiter is huge: you could fit 1,000 Earths into it
- **Weight**: Saturn is the lightest planet. It is believed if it were placed in a giant pond it would float because it's so light!
- **Divided**: Neptune has eight known moons but one of them, 'Triton', goes round Neptune in the opposite direction to the rest.

Full throttle

Deep impact

What you need
- Eggs or water balloons
- Cover-up and clean-up equipment

What you do
Choose a pair of volunteers and ask them to stand a metre apart. Give one an egg or water balloon and ask them to throw it to the other. Then move the pair two metres apart and ask them to do the same. The game ends when the egg/water balloon breaks! You might need to give more than one pair a chance to do this, as it might be a popular game!

Star songs

Reintroduce The Transporters and sing the *Space Academy* theme song, along with any actions. Sing a song that you have already sung at *Space Academy* and introduce a new one today.

One giant leap

This activity links to the Bible passage as it introduces the idea of strange communication.

Space communication

What you need
- Copies of the space code from page 91

What you do
Up front: write one of the messages below in the space code onto large sheets of paper (one copy per group) and get one group member to come to the front to act as scribe. Give each group a copy of the space code. The group members should shout out the letters to their scribe, who should then write it on their sheet of paper (if they can hear above the noise). The first one to finish is the winner.

1 We have touchdown!
2 One small step for man
3 Mayday! Mayday!
4 Make it so

Tell the story

For each Voyage, there are three options suggested for telling the Bible story: you can use the same approach each time, mix and match how you tell the story, or combine two or more approaches. Choose which will be most helpful for your team, your children and the style of your club.

1 The Space Commander now goes on to tell the Bible story based on Daniel 5 using their own words if possible (see page 7 for tips on how to do this). You can use the section headings, keywords and visual ideas from the script (see option 3) as memory joggers and to vary your story presentation each time.

2 Introduce today's episode from the *Space Academy* DVD. (If you are telling the story and using the DVD, tell the story first, then show the DVD so the children already have the outline of the events before seeing the episode.)

3 Or the Space Commander may prefer to follow the fully scripted retold Bible story for Voyage 4 on page 75.

Invisible writing

To give some idea of the impact of the writing on the wall, you can use an invisible writing method. For example, write the words, 'Number, Number, Weight, Divided' onto a large sheet of paper using a candle. When the time comes, paint over the words and the paint shouldn't stick where the candle wax is, making the words appear mysteriously. Be sure to practise this carefully, to make sure you get enough wax on the paper and that the paint is watery enough. If you are showing the words vertically on a 'wall' of some sort, do remember to protect the wall and floor where the paint may dribble. (You may know other ways to do invisible writing that work just as well.) It's probably better to use the English versions of the words written on the wall, but if you want to challenge the children a bit more, you could try using the Aramaic: Mene, mene, tekel, parsin.

Universe challenge

Before the session, put together some questions based on the space and astronaut facts the children heard earlier and the Bible passage for the day. You could include:

- How many Earths can you fit into Jupiter?
- Which of Neptune's moons goes round in the opposite direction to the rest?
- What did the king see that made him very frightened?
- Who was called for to unravel the mystery of the writing?

For today's scoring system have six bags with items of various weights in (marbles would work well for this, starting with just a couple in the first bag). The lightest bag will score 1, moving up gradually to the heaviest bag scoring 6. Hide these in the stage area. If a child answers correctly invite them to come up and look for a weighted bag. Have some scales to weigh them on and allocate the appropriate score.

Data check

Using the points below, spend a few moments summing up the teaching for the day.

- King Bel mocked God by using treasures from the Temple for his own banquet.
- God was angry with him and decided to teach him a lesson. (Remind the children of the hand writing the message on the wall and how this frightened the king.)
- Once again, God gave Daniel wisdom by revealing the meaning of the writing on the wall.
- King Bel had probably worshipped other gods before and nothing had happened. But here he discovered that God is real and powerful and that it matters how people treat him.
- Some people today also think that it doesn't matter what they do, and that God will let them off, but this story shows that God does mind. If we want to be like Daniel, not like the king, we need to remember to respect God and walk in his ways. But we know, too, that when we go wrong and admit it, God will forgive us.

Prayer

To conclude Action Stations! you may want to pause here to give the children an opportunity to think about what they've learnt and to pray silently. Before the session, create a 'space' prayer action that you can do just before you pray. You could say something like, 'Start to think about what God is like from what you've heard in this story – what would you want to say to him, right now? Because you can do that right now!' Make this time short as the children will probably only be quiet for a minute or so. Say 'Amen' or have another action so everyone knows it is the end of the prayer.

Lunar landing

45 minutes — small groups

During this time, remind the leaders to collect any questions for On the star spot and get them to the person being interviewed in plenty of time.

Cafe Cosmos

In your Starbase group, have your refreshments together and chat about the club so far. What are the children's favourite parts? Remind your group to think of questions to ask at On the star spot later. Remind them also of the space capsule, where they can leave their jokes and pictures. Go on to explore the Bible passage together more closely.

Bible discovery

With older children (8–10s)

Talk about parties you've been to recently and get the children to fill in their best party choice on page 28 of *Daniel's Data*. Read the introductory paragraph on page 29 and about what the king saw at his party from Daniel 5:5,6. Talk together about why it mattered that Belshazzar used the cups. Ask the children if they would have been afraid at the handwriting on the wall.

Get the children to complete the cartoon strip on pages 30–32. As they do so, make sure they have understood the story. (If necessary, read Daniel 5 from the Bible.) Invite the children to crack the code on page 33 to work out what the writing on the wall meant.

King Belshazzar found out that God is real and powerful – and that it matters how people treat him! Some people say that it doesn't matter what we do or that God will let us off – but this story shows that God does mind.

Ask the children what sort of things they should be careful about, if they want to be like Daniel, not like the king. Talk about what God wants and what God doesn't want.

End your time together by asking God to forgive you for anything that you have done which could make him angry. Thank God that he forgives us when we are sorry and tell him we are.

With younger children (5–7s)

Talk with the children about what parties they've been to, the food they like to eat at parties, etc. Then read Daniel 5 using a child-friendly Bible or retell it with your own words. Using *Star Sheet 4* invite the children to count up the number of hands and find the ten stolen gold cups at the feast. Talk about why it was wrong for the king to take the dishes and what God did to show him it was wrong.

Invite the children to find out the mystery message using the code.

The message reads: 'God wants you to be his friend and get to know him'. Ask the children if they've heard this message before and talk together about how they can be a friend of God. Talk about how we get to know God by spending time with him, listening, praying and reading the Bible. Also, explain to the children in a simple way that being God's friend means trusting in Jesus, and share something of what that means to you. If appropriate say a prayer together.

With all ages

Adapt these questions to suit your group, sharing your own feelings, opinions and experiences as appropriate:

- Have you ever borrowed things that you weren't supposed to? Did you get into trouble?
- Why do you think the king used the special cups from the Temple?
- Would you have been scared if you'd seen the handwriting on the wall?
- Would you like to have been there? Why – or why not?
- If you want to be like Daniel, not like the king, what sort of things should you be careful about?
- What is the difference between showing off (being boastful) and having a low estimate of your own importance (being humble)?
- If God wrote a message on the wall to you, what would you like it to say?

Shuttlecraft

Choose a construction activity from page 69. For extra craft ideas, see *Ultimate Craft* (SU, 978 1 84427 364 5).

Fit for space

Check that your astronauts are fit for space by choosing a games activity from page 70. For extra games ideas, see *Ultimate Games* (SU, 978 1 84427 365 2).

Red alert!

25 minutes — all together

Space capsule

Welcome everyone back together by playing the *Space Academy* theme song. Read out some of the messages

VOYAGE 4 **THE HEAVENLY HAND**

and pictures from the space capsule. Thank all the contributing astronauts and remind everyone to bring in more jokes and pictures tomorrow.

Star songs
The Transporters lead the children in a couple of lively songs.

Data recall
The Captain rounds up what the Starbases have been exploring together, recapping the following points:
- King Belshazzar disobeys God.
- God is angry and teaches him a lesson.
- The advisors can't work out the mystery.
- God gives Daniel wisdom to solve it.
- The king is dethroned and a new king takes his place.
- We need to remember how great and powerful God is and that we need to respect him.

Cosmic code
Today, recap verse 6 of the Learn and remember verse by using the following actions:
- **Remember**: tap your head a couple of times
- **The Lord**: point upwards
- **In everything**: bring hands around an imaginary globe
- **You**: point to each other
- **Do**: bring one fist down on the other
- **And he will**: move both hands outwards from chest
- **Show you**: look around with eyes wide open
- **The right**: do an imaginary tick
- **Way**: march on the spot.

Alternatively, you may prefer to use British sign language or Makaton, if you have someone who is familiar with these.

On the star spot
Interview one of the Lieutenants or Ensign about how it feels to be forgiven by God when they have done something wrong and said 'sorry'. Link this to Jesus' death on the cross. Bring in the truth that no one is beyond forgiveness, no matter what they have done – and everyone needs God's forgiveness, even if they haven't done anything awful. It may be possible to have two contrasting interviews with a team member who has followed Jesus for as long as they can remember and another who had a more conscious start to their faith-relationship, both answering: 'What does this mean to you today?'

Also include the question you have picked out from those the children thought of; invite them to ask their question and give them their 'prize'. When you have finished, thank the Lieutenant or assistant for being On the star spot!

Drama: The final frontier
Introduce the next episode of the comedy-drama, 'The final frontier'. In today's episode the crew are put in a life-threatening situation on board the Starship (insert name of club/town). Will they be able to come up with a plan in time? Who is behind this evil plot to destroy them? Let's find out.

Final orbit
Round off Red alert! by asking the children what they have enjoyed at *Space Academy* today and then include those things in a short prayer of thanks, using your space prayer action.

Encourage the children to come back tomorrow by saying something similar to the following:

'What a great time we've had today. But there's more in store for us tomorrow. Will the new king in the Bible story accept Daniel's God or not? What will the crew of the Starship (Name) find on the last planet in the Delta Quadrant? What more mind-mashing messages will Buzz have for his astronauts, and will the Cosmic code all fit into place? Come back tomorrow to find out!'

Sing the *Space Academy* theme song and send the astronauts back to their Starbases to round off the day's session.

Touchdown
10 minutes **small groups**

Creative prayer
Admire the rings the group have made (if this was your chosen craft) and let this lead into thinking about the story. Talk about how powerful God is. He knew each person in the story and what was going to happen to them.

Look at the fingerprints again, remembering that God knows us, too. Take turns to pick one up and pray for that person to get to know God better. Let the children take their own fingerprint home.

Voyage clear-up
30 minutes **team time**

After all the children have gone, clear up from the day's events and set up for the next session, if the premises you are using makes that feasible. Meet together as a team to debrief. Use a feedback system that works best for you – there is an evaluation form on the *Space Academy* website. This would be the time for the Fleet admiral to raise any obvious issues. Also raise anything that has cropped up that needs sorting before tomorrow and assign someone to sort it out. Remember to praise the team for the things that went well and urge them to do as well or better tomorrow! Have a brief time of prayer where Lieutenants and Ensigns can pray for their groups, and other team members can pray for their areas of responsibility. If you have the time and the facilities, you may wish to share a meal together.

CAPTAIN'S LOG 4

SPACE ACADEMY

PHOTOCOPIABLE PAGE

Star sheet Voyage 4
The heavenly hand

Bible fun with a friend or on your own.

TRAINEE'S LOG 4

1 How many hands can you count here?

2 What mystery message is the hand writing here? Use the code to find out.

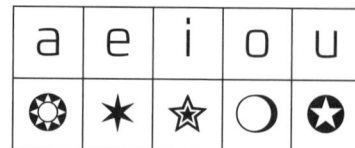

a	e	i	o	u
✹	★	☆	○	⊛

G_o_d w_a_nts y_o_ _u_ to b_e_ h_i_s fr_i_ _e_nd _a_nd g_e_t to kn_o_w h_i_m.

3 Can you find ten stolen gold cups at the feast?

Voyage 5
In the pit

Key passage
Daniel 6

Key storylines
- Daniel's enemies persuade King Darius to make a law that says people must only pray to him for the next 30 days.
- Daniel prays to God, as he always does, and his enemies tell the king.
- The king has no choice but to obey his own law and has Daniel put into a pit of lions. God keeps him safe.
- In the morning, Darius is relieved and has Daniel brought out of the pit; he calls on everyone to worship God.

Key aims
- To find out what happened when Daniel risked his life by praying to God – and how God answered his prayers and the prayers of the king.
- To realise that God answered Daniel's faithful prayers and the prayer of the non-believing king and to work out what that means for us today.
- To experience a dramatic final day of the holiday club programme together and to encourage the children to return for your closing Sunday service and other future events (depending on what you are planning).

For children with no church background
Of all the stories in Daniel, this is probably the best known, but if the children know the story they will probably only remember the lions, so be sure to explain why Daniel was put there: he had done nothing wrong, but the king was tricked into having him thrown there. Daniel would have known what would happen if he prayed so openly, but he still continued. We don't have to be afraid to pray, and the Bible assures us that God will listen!

For church children
It would be easy to tell children used to church that the worst that might happen to them for praying openly would be that they are mocked by those who don't believe in it. But this in itself is awful for a child! So focus their attention on the amazing fact that they can pray to God anywhere and at any time, and he will listen, and encourage them to talk to God about everything.

For children of other faiths
Set times for prayer is a familiar concept for children of other faiths and they would understand both the times and postures undertaken by Daniel. You may want to explain that they can pray to God at any time and he will hear their prayer. It may be appropriate to explain how Daniel probably knew this but wanted to explain an important truth to those watching him. He was a law-abiding person (as an important official of the government he must have been) but there were things he would not compromise on and his faith was one such thing.

For children with additional needs
Encourage each child to pray; even with no voice, let the child know that God can hear inside our heads. A child might hold a 'prayer ball' and at the end you could join in with an 'Amen'.

Don't underestimate what God is doing and how children are responding prayerfully.

'A smile during a song for the first time may be a step of faith. Touching someone's arm quite deliberately during prayers may be an important response to God's love… These small responses are as valid as reciting a creed for someone for whom doctrine is difficult to comprehend.'
Lowe, A, *Evangelism and Learning Disability*, Grove (1998)

CAPTAIN'S LOG 4

Lieutenants' briefing
Spiritual preparation

Read together
Read Daniel 6:1–5,10.

Explore together
Prepare today with some of the ideas you'll be using later with the children. Read verse 10 and see if you can find five things it says about Daniel talking to God. When Daniel heard the king's new order had been signed he went to pray. Surely he didn't have to go home, and pray towards Jerusalem? He could have prayed secretly or silently. Consider how Daniel's life was full of prayer and how God answered his prayers – in this story and in the others you have been reading in *Space Academy*.

Talk about how and why Daniel was kept safe. God is powerful and he keeps faith with those, like Daniel, who keep faith with him – but look again at the Bible passage to see what part Darius played. He signed the law in the first place but he also prayed for Daniel's safety, even though he did not believe in God! His prayers were answered, too.

Run through the aims for the day (those listed on page 59 and others that you have chosen for the club), and think through and chat informally about how these are going to be met through the time together.

Reflect together
Aspects of Daniel's story are so contemporary: a man who is good at his job, capable, honest, faithful to God – and instead of being appreciated for these qualities, they inspire jealousy and resentment. Think of other Bible people who generate a similar reaction – Paul, Peter, John the Baptist – and, of course, Jesus. When others oppose us, we need to know who we can really trust: what does the story of Daniel show us about trusting God?

Daniel's colleagues couldn't find anything to accuse him of except praying to God. How about us? Share a time when God answered your prayers or a time when a non-Christian was made aware of something about God through your lifestyle. Do the people around you know that you are a Christian? Is it easy to tell from your life? Are the children at *Space Academy* seeing your faith in action as well as hearing you talk about it?

Pray together
Pray that the team and children would realise the vital importance of talking to God in prayer. Pray also that the things the children have learnt would have a lasting impact on their lives. Pray for each other, for good relationships within the team, for stamina, boldness, patience and to be good examples to the children.

Practical preparation
Talk through your programme together, remind everyone of the programme and who is doing what, ensuring that everyone knows their part in the day and has everything they need.

Set up the different areas of the club and make sure that everything is in place in plenty of time, so you are ready as the first children come from the registration area.

Listen to any last minute information or instructions from your Fleet admiral.

Share a 'team booster' before heading into the club. (For example, stand closely in a circle, with one arm out and touching hands with everyone else; say together 'Be bold, be strong, for the Lord our God is with us.')

Remember to smile!

What you need checklist

- **Registration** Registration forms, badges, labels, pens, team lists
- **Starbases** Bibles, *Daniel's Data* or *Star Sheets*, Bible discovery notes
- **Music** The Transporters band or backing tracks
- **Drama** Costumes and props
- **Technology** PA system, laptop, PowerPoints and projection/OHP and acetates, *Space Academy* DVD
- **Activities** Equipment for games and construction
- **The Captain** Running order, notes, Full throttle and One giant leap equipment, quiz questions and props
- **The Space Commander** Story script
- **Café Cosmos** Drinks and biscuits or other refreshments

Space programme
As the children arrive and register, play some space-related or sci-fi music (such as *Star Trek*, *Star Wars* or *Dr Who*) and display the *Space Academy* logo on the screen to welcome the children.

Have a welcome team on hand to take the children to their groups. Encourage the group leaders to be ready to welcome the children in their groups.

Report to starbase
10 minutes small groups
'Remember to pray' card

What you need
- A6 landscape sheets of card (one per child) with words 'Remember to pray' in outline writing
- Felt pens
- Wooden clothes pags

What you do
Welcome the children and give each one a 'Remember to pray' card. As they colour them in, chat to them about what they have enjoyed most about *Space Academy*. Write names on the backs of the cards and collect them up for later.

Action stations
45 minutes all together

Play the *Space Academy* theme song as a sign for the children to join the larger group. The Captain should welcome everyone to *Space Academy*. Check to see if anyone can remember what they've learnt about Daniel so far.

Phaser-fitness
Super Nova should lead the workout, using moves from the previous days.

VOYAGE 5 **IN THE PIT**

Invite some volunteers to come and help lead the workout. Introduce some 'prowling around as lions' moves today. Everyone needs to be super fit to face the challenges of life on a spaceship!

Brain boosters

The Captain says how today's story takes you to a dark, cold and dangerous place. Buzz walks in unannounced in a big coat, carrying a flash torch and some kind of hazard sign. The Captain asks him why he's dressed like that. Buzz explains that our space facts will reveal all…

1 'Houston we've had a problem.' These were the words of James Lovell, an astronaut on the Apollo 13 mission in 1970. An explosion on the spacecraft led to the loss of the main power supply. The astronauts battled with water shortage, extreme cold, a build-up of carbon dioxide and the problem of how to get back to earth with limited power. Despite everything, they made it back, although they had to abandon their goal of landing on the moon.

2 Another very dark and cold place is the 'dwarf' planet Pluto. 'Dwarf' because it's much smaller than the other planets. It's also the planet furthest away from Earth and has not yet been visited by a spacecraft so not much is known about it. We do know that it's in perpetual darkness as it's so far from the sun and the surface temperature varies between about -235° C and -210° C. Buzz ends by saying 'I think I'll need more than my coat and torch to go there.'

Full throttle

Space buggy

What you need
- Plate of custard (or other runny, messy food)
- Cover-up and clean-up equipment

What you do
Choose a pair of volunteers and tell them they're going to run a wheelbarrow race. After they have got into the 'wheelbarrow' formation, produce the plate of custard and place it on the barrow's back. The team have to get to the end of a course and back without spilling any of the custard (you could clear a course through the children, so that they can cheer the volunteers all the way). You could run this as a race between two pairs.

Star songs

Reintroduce The Transporters and sing the *Space Academy* theme song, along with any actions. Sing a song that you have already sung at *Space Academy* and maybe introduce a new one today.

One giant leap

This activity links to the theme of the Bible passage as it introduces the idea of asking for and receiving.

Captain's orders

What you need
- List of items readily available to the teams (eg, a sock, a coin, a watch, a Bible – include some more obscure things, such as 'someone who speaks French' or 'a person with a birthday in May')

What you do
Everyone can join in this game but be warned, it can get rather chaotic! Station a few leaders around the room. Once an item is called, a child can take it to one of those leaders, who will check it and then signal that they have that item. Give the first child to bring each item a sweet or a point for their team.

Tell the story

For each Voyage, there are three options suggested for telling the Bible story: you can use the same approach each time, mix and match how you tell the story, or combine two or more approaches. Choose which will be most helpful for your team, your children and the style of your club.

1 The Space Commander now goes on to tell the Bible story based on Daniel 6, using their own words if possible (see page 7 for tips on how to do this). You can use the section headings and sound effects from the script (see option 3) as memory joggers and to vary your story presentation each time.

2 Introduce today's episode from the *Space Academy* DVD. (If you are telling the story and using the DVD, tell the story first, then show the DVD so the children already have the outline of the events before seeing the episode.)

3 Or the Space Commander may prefer to follow the fully scripted retold Bible story for Voyage 5 on page 76.

Sound effects

Set up some responses with the children. Every time you say 'Daniel' they have to cheer, 'Hooray!' Every time you say 'enemies' they boo, 'Boo!' Every time you say 'king' they have to say, 'Your majesty!' Every time you say 'plan', they have to say 'Dun, da, dun, dun, duuunn!' And every time you say 'lions', they have to roar! The script shows the response words in bold.

Universe challenge

Before the session, put together some questions based on the space and astronaut facts the children heard earlier and the Bible passage for the day. You could include:
- What space mission was nearly a disaster?
- What planet is in perpetual darkness?
- What law did the king make?
- What did Daniel continue to do even though the law forbade it?

For today's scoring system, make a 'planetarium' using a large sheet of black card with white paint splatter-painted on it to look like stars. Also paint in some star patterns that make up the numbers 1 to 6. Cover over each number with a piece of black card, attaching it along one edge to act as a hinge. If a child answers correctly invite them to come up and lift up one of the flaps to reveal their score on the background.

Data check

Using the points below, spend a few moments summing up the teaching for the day.
- Calling out to God: Being so committed to God placed Daniel in a spot of bother. He had refused to give in to the demands of the king, so he was thrown into a den of lions. However, the king recognised Daniel's commitment to his God, and on Daniel's behalf called out to God to save him. And God did!
- Following God in all situations: It must have been really hard for Daniel to stand up against the

CAPTAIN'S LOG 4

king in order to follow his God. But he knew that this was the only way and he never gave up. He gave his life to God and was committed to him even through the difficult times.

- God wants us to follow him too. We are very unlikely to end up in a den of lions, but we will all face difficulties at some point in our lives. But God has promised that when we call out to him in prayer, he will listen and answer. He will be with us in every situation; he will give us the strength and patience to stay close to him and to live a life which follows him.

Prayer

To conclude Action Stations! you may want to pause here to give the children an opportunity to think about what they've learnt and to pray silently. Before the session, create a 'space' prayer action that you can do just before you pray. You could say something like, 'Start to think about what God is like from what you've heard in this story – what would you want to say to him, right now? Because you can do that right now!' Make this time short as the children will probably only be quiet for a minute or so. Say 'Amen' or have another action so everyone knows it is the end of the prayer.

Lunar landing

45 minutes small groups

During this time, remind the leaders to collect any questions for On the star spot and get them to the person being interviewed in plenty of time.

Cafe Cosmos

In your Starbase group, have your refreshments together and chat about the club. What are the children's favourite parts? Remind your group to think of questions to ask at On the star spot later. Remind them also of the space capsule, where they can leave their jokes and pictures. Go on to explore the Bible passage together more closely.

Bible discovery

With older children (8-10s)

Talk about what it would be like to be in charge of this country and what they would change. Encourage the children to draw pictures of the things they would change on page 35 of *Daniel's Data* and ask them if they think they would be good at being in charge. Read the introductory paragraph on page 36 and then Daniel 6:6–9. Ask the children if they think Daniel would obey the new law and what would happen if he didn't. Read verse 10 on page 37 together and then encourage the children to fill in the five things it says about Daniel talking to God and to circle the words that describe Daniel. Invite the children to put the six things that happened next on the bar graph on page 38. Read the final part of the story on page 39 and encourage the children to circle the words that describe Daniel. Talk about how and why Daniel was kept safe.

Get the children to crack the code on page 40 and talk about whether they were surprised it was Darius who said these praise words. Get the children to draw the stick-people praying in different ways. Talk about how Daniel's life was full of prayer and how God answered his prayers. If appropriate, share a time when God answered your prayers or a time when a non-Christian was made aware of something about God through your lifestyle. Ask the children about how they pray and encourage them to fill in page 41 on their own.

End the session by thanking God for all that you have learnt about Daniel this week at *Space Academy* and asking him to help you live for him and stay close to him, as Daniel did.

With younger children (5-7s)

Read Daniel 6 to the children as expressively as you can! If you have an imaginative group, you might get the children to come up with sound effects to make as you read. Encourage the children to complete the maze on *Star Sheet 5*. Then talk about why Daniel still prayed to God, even though he would be in big danger!

Talk about the importance of prayer in our own lives and chat about things we can pray about such as holidays, illness, friends etc. Fill in the promise at the bottom of the *Star Sheet* (God always hears me when I pray to him) using the letters they haven't used yet.

Ask the children to pick one thing to pray for and encourage them to say a simple prayer out loud for this. A simple way to do this is to pass a small object around like a toy lion (cuddly toy or plastic zoo/wildlife animal), and when the person holds it they say a short prayer before passing it on to the next person. When you've finished, all say together 'God always hears me when I pray to him'.

With all ages

Adapt these questions to suit your group, sharing your own feelings, opinions and experiences as appropriate:

- Do you have any fears: eg, of animals?
- What things have you done that you were scared about doing: eg, abseiling, high ropes, theme park ride?
- Depending on what you have discussed so far, think about where God fits into those situations.
- How do you think Daniel felt when he was thrown into the lions' den?
- Why was it important for Daniel to pray to God?
- Did you notice that King Darius prayed as well? He did not believe in God so why did he pray – and why did God answer his prayer?
- How do you think the king's other advisers felt when they found out Daniel was still alive in the morning?
- If you could be anyone from this story, who would you be? Why?
- What is God like in this story? How do you think and feel about him now? Has that changed since the start of *Space Academy*?

Shuttlecraft

Choose a construction activity from page 69. For extra craft ideas, see *Ultimate Craft* (SU, 978 1 84427 364 5).

Fit for space

Check that your astronauts are fit for space by choosing a games activity from page 70. For extra games ideas, see *Ultimate Games* (SU, 978 1 84427 365 2).

VOYAGE 5 **IN THE PIT**

Red alert!
25 minutes
all together

Space capsule
Welcome everyone back together by playing the *Space Academy* theme song. Read out some of the messages and pictures from the space capsule. Thank all the contributing astronauts for putting their messages, codes, jokes and pictures in the space capsule this week.

Star songs
The Transporters lead the children in a couple of lively songs.

Data recall
The Captain rounds up what the Starbases have been exploring together, recapping the following points:
- Daniel's enemies wanted to harm him because he loved God.
- Daniel was faithful and risked his life by praying to God.
- God protected him and rescued him.
- God answered his prayers and the prayers of the king.
- God is living, powerful and saves his followers.
- God answers our prayers today.

Cosmic code
Today, see if any of the children can remember both parts of the Learn and remember verse. In advance, write out just the key words from Proverbs 3:5,6 onto individual sheets of fluorescent paper or card and hide them around the room. Explain that you need a volunteer from each Starbase to find the main words from the verses that are hidden around the room. When all the sheets are found and put in order, shout out the words on the sheets and whisper the words that come in between. Then do it the other way around! Finish by discarding all the sheets and trying to say the complete verses without any clues.

On the star spot
Make the most of this key moment to describe how Daniel's experience is paralleled in the lives of people today and how significant it is to have a relationship with Jesus. Interview one of the Lieutenants or Ensigns about a time when they were under pressure to not follow Jesus. Include asking what they think is the best thing about Jesus. Or you could ask them about how prayer makes a difference in their lives.

Also include the question you have picked out from those the children thought of; invite the child to come up and ask their question and give them their 'prize'. When you have finished, thank the Lieutenant or Ensign for being On the star spot!

Drama: The final frontier
Introduce the final episode of the comedy-drama, 'The final frontier'. The crew have one final mission to spread the good news of Mission Command, with goodness, kindness, generosity, honesty and mercy. This time they venture to the planet Notalivestar where something rather unexpected happens.

Final orbit
Round off Red alert! by asking the children what they have enjoyed at *Space Academy* today and at the whole club and then include those things in a short prayer of thanks, using your space prayer action. Thank all the astronauts for being part of *Space Academy* and remind them of the Sunday service if you are having one.

Sing the *Space Academy* theme song and send the astronauts back to their Starbases to round off the day's session.

Touchdown
10 minutes
small groups

Creative prayer
Talk together about the story and remind the children that Daniel didn't just start to pray when he was confronted by hungry lions. It was a lifelong habit he had got into, and a very good one for the children to start too. Give out the 'Remember to pray' cards from earlier and help the children fix a wooden clothes peg to the back with strong glue or double-sided tape. Ask the children where they will display their card to remind them to pray – and what sorts of things they will pray about. Assure them that you will be praying for them, too, as they leave *Space Academy*.

Voyage clear-up
30 minutes
team time

After all the children have gone, clear up from the day's events. You may need to have an extended clear-up session if you are not using the venue again. Meet together as a team to debrief and make sure everyone knows the plan for the Sunday service, if you are having one. The Fleet admiral may like to spend some time thanking everyone for taking part. Have a brief time of prayer where everyone together prays for the whole club, thanking God for what he has done and lifting up all the children. If you have the time and the facilities, you may wish to share a meal together.

CAPTAIN'S LOG 4

Star sheet Voyage 5
In the pit

Bible fun with a friend or on your own.

1 Can you find a way for Daniel to escape from the lions? What does he have to do to be safe?

2 Colour in every square with a **q**, **x** or **z** to read the message.

x	G	q	o	z	d	q	x	a	l	z	w	z	x	a	q	y	q
z	s	x	h	e	z	x	a	q	r	x	z	s	q	z	m	x	e
w	q	h	x	e	z	x	n	z	q	l	z	p	x	r	z	x	a
q	y	x	z	t	x	o	z	q	h	x	q	z	i	x	z	m	q

3 We can pray to God about anything. What do you want to pray about today? Write it in the speech bubble.

Re-entry Sunday service 2
Back to Earth?

CAPTAIN'S LOG 4

Key passage
Daniel 1–6 (as a round-up of the whole adventure)

Key storylines
- God is with his people, wherever they are.
- Daniel and his friends stood firm for God and lived God's way, no matter what the circumstances: we can learn from their example of boldness and quiet courage.
- God did not let them down: we can learn from their example of faith and trust.

Key aim
To remind all the children of what they have learnt in the holiday club and to share those things with their parents and the wider church family.

For children with no church background
Children who have come all week still often find it a bit of a shock coming to church on Sunday. They may expect it to be the same as the holiday club, but no matter how hard we try, if it is a church service it will seem very different to them. Early in the service make sure familiar friends are involved and familiar activities included. Make it as much part of the holiday club as you can.

For church children
These children are used to church – so surprise them by how much like the holiday club it is. Make it the best service they have ever been to! Be sure to include as many of their favourite things from the holiday club as you can – at least songs, verses and fun stuff, as well as the Bible input on Daniel and his friends.

For children of other faiths
Encourage the children to invite their families to this service. Use the word 'families' rather than parents as many Asian families operate as a family unit and can be quite large. So don't be surprised if the whole family comes along (parents, siblings, aunties, grandpa, etc). Have people of different ages ready to welcome them. Make sure they have seats, especially the adults, so that they feel welcomed. Think carefully about how to follow up with these children and their families and have people on hand to build friendships with them. Invite them to other appropriate events (parents and toddlers, old people's day club, etc).

For children with additional needs
Think about the family situations. Now that you have a good relationship with the chid, how can you, as a church or as an individual, support the family in the future? This could be through babysitting, providing meals, washing, shopping or being a befriender in a regular children's group.

Service outline

You will need
Cards numbered 1–9, each with an answer to a quiz question on it (take care not to give the answers the same numbers as the questions) and nine volunteers for the quiz scoring system; jigsaw pictures of the various Daniel stories; cards, PowerPoint or acetates with the letters T,R,U,S,T written so everyone can see them; a blindfold; a strong adult volunteer who has been briefed about the trust exercise.

Welcome
The family service provides the opportunity for some of the craft and Starbase material from the week to be displayed. Assemble the gallery of work in the entrance as people come in to the church, or in an area where you might serve refreshments. Ensure you have team members at the door to welcome holiday club children and their families to the church, and show them where everything is. This will help people feel at ease as they enter a building they may not be familiar with. It may be helpful to your regular congregation to have the welcome done by someone who regularly leads services, and to allow the Captain and the Space Commander to lead other parts. Begin with an appropriate well-known song or hymn.

Star songs
Sing two or three songs that you have been singing at *Space Academy*, including the theme song. Have The Transporters lead these, if they are available. If you have been using action songs, get some volunteer astronauts to help with the actions. In all your music for this service, you'll need to strike a balance between children and adults, and church and non-church people. Try to be as inclusive as you can.

Introductory activity
The Captain should welcome everyone to today's voyage. They should give a brief overview of the week's activities (but not talking about the content of the Bible narratives) by interviewing one or two astronauts. They should then turn the things that have been especially mentioned into a prayer of thanks, but also include things that will have been good for people not involved in *Space Academy*.

Cosmic code
Explain that, as part of their training at *Space Academy*, the astronauts (children) have been learning a Bible verse that speaks about trusting God. Ask if there are any astronauts here who can remember the verse for the week. Hopefully you'll have some children willing to have a go so invite a few of them to come up together and recite it to the rest of the congregation. Put the verse up on the screen as a PowerPoint slide and help the congregation to learn it. After repeating it a few times, gradually 'dissolve' some of the words on the screen until only a few are left as memory joggers. Give a small prize to the children who had a go at reciting the verse.

Universe challenge
Choose nine volunteers and give each a numbered card to hold so that the congregation can see the numbers.

Divide the congregation into two teams and ask questions in turn. Instead of giving the answer to the question, they should select a number at random; the person holding that number then reads out the answer on the back. If it is correct, the person sits down and the team scores a point. If incorrect, the next question is asked of the other team, but of course the place of one answer is now known. Initially this system means that anyone can answer a question, whether on science, the Bible narrative or events at *Space Academy*. As the quiz continues, it becomes a question of remembering where answers are hidden.

Questions:
1. Where were Daniel and his friends taken? **Babylon**
2. Name one of Daniel's friends (either Jewish or Babylonian name). **Hanaiah/Shadrach, Mishael/Meshach, Azariah/Abednego**
3. Which planet is 57 million miles from the earth? **Mercury**
4. What did Buzz Brain have for breakfast? **Sprouts**
5. What metal did King Nebuchadnezzar use to make his statue? **Gold**
6. What is the name of the fitness instructor in *Space Academy*? **Super Nova**
7. Where did Daniel go to pray when he heard that praying to God was no longer allowed? **Upstairs room where windows faced Jerusalem**
8. In space, what is known as 'the eye of God'? **Helix nebula**
9. In the *Space Academy* drama, what was the name of the 'baddie'? **Odor**
10. What did King Darius say about God? **That he is the Living God/he rescues people**

One giant leap
Explain that at *Space Academy* each day you've invited several people to come to the front to take part in a challenge that is messy, fast-paced and lots of fun! Reassure people that today's challenge isn't messy but involves trust. Ask if there is anyone here who thinks they can trust you. Blindfold the volunteer and stand behind them about an arm's length away; tell them where you are. (NB If you are using PA and the sound therefore comes from the speakers, you will need to speak to them momentarily without the microphone, so that they know where you are.) On a count of three, ask the person to fall back into your arms. If they don't feel able to, you should ask for another volunteer. Once they have fallen and you have caught them, stand them up again and move to stand in front of them, once again speaking momentarily without PA so they know you are now in front of them. As you do this, indicate to a pre-briefed assistant to quietly stand where you were behind the volunteer. Ask the volunteer if they trust you; assure them that they will be caught, and invite them to fall back. Whether they succeed in doing this or not, say that everyone will be finding out in a bit the significance of this trust game.

Space awards

Say that at the end of any 'academy' or training course, students are often given some kind of award. Have a crazy prize-giving with awards for children and leaders for unusual things they have done: the messiest leader; the science expert; the cosmic café star, etc. You could give out badges or certificates with the *Space Academy* logo and the award title on it. Or you could award confectionery with suitable names like Galaxy, Mars bars, Starburst, Milky Way, etc. During the awards you could have suitable space-themed music playing in the background. Encourage the congregation to take part by clapping those who receive awards. Remember to thank the whole team and all the astronauts for taking part too.

Tell the story

The Bible input for this service is a recap of all the stories that we have had during the holiday club week. It may seem to some of the church that you have been on another planet, but the children will be with you. Get them to help you whizz through all the stories, making the connecting link the way in which Daniel and his friends trusted God in each situation and saw God doing amazing things for them and through them.

To help with this recap, make up a jigsaw puzzle of the five stories. (This could be done as a PowerPoint presentation or draw simple pictures, mounted on cardboard and stuck on a felt board using Velcro.) Put a piece in place each time you summarise that story, so that the whole builds up to a composite picture of the first six chapters of Daniel.

Having reminded everyone of the stories, highlight one word that sums up each of the narratives as follows:

Chapter 1 **Tested**

Chapter 2 **Revealed**

Chapter 3 **Unharmed**

Chapter 5 **Slain**!

Chapter 6 **Trusting**

You may want to have the initial letters on cards or down the left side of a PowerPoint or OHP slide. They do, of course, spell out the word 'TRUST'; talk about the amazing way that Daniel and his friends trusted God even when things were incredibly hard for them, and their lives were threatened.

Life may not be quite so hard for us, but each of us will go through things we find especially difficult: perhaps starting at a new school, or coping with illness for ourselves or someone we love; perhaps feeling alone when someone dies, or rejected when we lose our job; maybe it's hard being teased or bullied; having to move away from family and friends to start at university. Whatever it is, we know from Daniel's experiences that God will never leave us nor let us down; we must learn to trust him to help and direct us.

Trust is believing something or someone utterly, no matter what. Refer back to the trust exercise they saw earlier. Comment on how the volunteer couldn't see the 'catcher' but had to trust in what they said would happen. Explain that it's like that with God. Although we can't see him, he is there and is utterly trustworthy. Say that it probably wasn't easy for the volunteer to trust and that it is hard to trust when things are tough, but the Bible – and Daniel's story in particular – shows us that God is faithful and strong. Lead a short prayer thanking God for who he is, and asking for the courage to trust him always.

Space capsule

Before the service, put the names (and photos) of people known to the congregation, who are struggling with hard times, onto individual sheets of paper. Post these in the space capsule. Explain that the space capsule doesn't have jokes in today but the names of people who are struggling. Invite some children to come up and take out one sheet each and read it out (they may need help with difficult names). Say that you're now going to lead everyone in a short prayer for these people. If appropriate, use the prayer action you've been using this week, explaining it first to the congregation.

Prayer

Say a simple prayer including the names of the people on the sheets and for everyone present with things they find difficult, ending the prayer with these words:

Leader: When things are tough,

All: Help me to trust you.

Leader: When the way is rough,

All: Help me to trust you.

Leader: When I feel I've had enough,

All: Help me to trust you.

Leader: For you, God, are powerful, faithful, trustworthy, loving and always there for me.

All: Amen.

Final orbit

Thank everyone for coming and end with an appropriate song and a last enthusiastic rendition of the theme song.

SPACE ACADEMY

CAPTAIN'S LOG 5

Resource bank

The engine room

Here in the engine room you'll find many of the resources you need for *Space Academy*: the scripts for telling the Bible story; craft and game ideas including templates and diagrams; the theme song and Learn and remember verse song; the Bible discovery notes and the 'Final Frontier' drama. You can photocopy those pages marked 'Photocopiable'. For all other resources go to www.scriptureunion.org.uk/spaceacademy.

Construction/craft

In this section you'll find a craft idea for each day of the club and a couple of extra ideas. Some of the craft supplies mentioned may be difficult to come by in local shops but the more obscure ones are available on the internet.

Try Baker Ross for A5 scratch art sheets and stick-on magnetic discs for 'Fruity veggie magnets'; acrylic rings and stick-on jewels for 'Bling rings' and wiggle eyes for 'Lion pots'. 'Hope' educational supplies have the double-sided foil (Metal decorations) on their website. IKEA often have cheap picture frames, and small flowerpots should be easy to obtain in somewhere like Wilkinsons.

Voyage 1

Fruity veggie magnets

What you need
- A5 sheets of scratch art card
- Fruit and vegetable templates
- Scratch sticks (or use cocktail sticks)
- Pencils
- Scissors
- Stick-on magnets or magnetic tape

What you do
Draw round as many fruit and vegetable templates as will fit on the card and cut them out. (Have the shapes cut out ready for younger children.) Templates are available on page 89. The children can use the offcuts to practise scraping away the top layer with a cocktail stick to reveal the colours underneath. Then they can decorate the fruit and vegetable shapes. When these are finished, fix a magnet to the back of each one. Write the child's name or initials on the back of their shape.

Voyage 2

Soap carving

What you need
- Bars of soap (these can be bought in bulk quite cheaply at supermarkets or cash-and-carry warehouses)
- Wooden kebab sticks

What you do
Show the children how easily the soap can be carved by scraping with the kebab stick. Suggest they spend a little while thinking about the design of their carving and perhaps drawing it lightly on the soap before starting properly. A good way is to make a simple shape such as a butterfly or their initial and then scrape away the soap around it, leaving the shape in relief. Make the connection with today's story being about a statue and that often statues are carved out of wood or metal.

Be warned – this can get very addictive and you may end up with piles of soap flakes and no carvings, but it's great fun!

Voyage 3

Flame frames

What you need
- Small picture frames (for safety use ones with Perspex rather than glass)
- Red, yellow and orange card
- Pens or pencils
- Scissors
- Double-sided tape
- (Optional) photos of the children (if you have the facilities to do this) to fit inside the frames

What you do
Help the children to draw flame shapes on the card. If you wish use the templates from page 89. Cut out the shapes and arrange them around the edge of the frame. When you are satisfied with the arrangement fix them down one at a time with double-sided tape. Write 'God' or 'Jesus' in the centre of the backing card. Give the children their own photo or suggest that they find a picture of themselves to put in the frame over the top of 'Jesus' or 'God'. It will remind them of the story: that God is powerful and is always with them even if they can't see him.

Voyage 4

Bling rings

What you need
- Acetate sheet
- Clear double-sided tape
- Scissors
- OHP pens in bright colours
- Stick-on jewels

What you do
Make the connection with today's story as the king offered Daniel power, royal robes and 'bling' – a gold chain around his neck. Say that your 'bling' won't be a gold chain but a ring.

For each ring cut a strip of acetate about 8 cm long and 1.5–2 cm wide. Put a small piece of double-sided tape in the centre. Cut a circle or oval shape (3–4 cm across) from acetate and fix this to the tape. Decorate the shape and the band of the ring by creating patterns using the pens and by sticking on the jewels. Be aware that some of the band will overlap eventually. When the ring is decorated fix another piece of tape to one end of the band. Wrap the ring around the preferred finger and fix with the tape.

Although this seems quite a 'girlie' activity, boys can be reminded that men often wear signet rings with an initial on a little finger. Ready-made transparent acrylic rings are available from craft catalogues. These can be decorated in a similar way.

Voyage 5

Lion pots

What you need
- Small plastic plant pots
- Template of outside of pot (see page 89 for template for 80 mm pot)
- Yellow paper
- Glue
- Scissors
- Pens
- Wiggle eyes
- Yellow tissue paper
- (Optional) compost and cress or grass seed

What you do
Draw round the template on the yellow paper and cut out the shape (or have these ready cut out). Glue this carefully around the outside of the pot. Stick two wiggle eyes fairly close together on the pot and draw the lion's nose and a mouth with sharp teeth. Cut some strips of tissue paper in short sections and fringe along one edge. Stick these around the face to make the lion's mane.

If you want your lion to eventually disappear into the jungle, fill the pot with compost and sprinkle cress or grass seeds on it. Don't forget to water it, but be careful to avoid getting water on the paper!

Extra craft ideas

Hubble space telescope

What you need
- Card roll (such as kitchen towel roll)
- Lolly sticks
- Grey marker pens
- Tin foil
- Orange or brown card or thick paper
- Glue
- Scissors
- String or fishing line (if you want to hang your telescope)

What you do
Colour in the lolly stick using the grey marker pen. Take the card roll and cut two slits from the top down parallel to each other. Make each slit about two-thirds down the roll. (Children may need help with this.) Insert your craft stick evenly into the slits. Tear some long strips of tin foil and cover your card roll, working around the craft sticks. The foil should just stay in place, but add a dab of glue here and there if needed. From card or thick paper, Cut two 10 cm squares and fold them in half. These rectangles will be the solar panels on the side of the telescope.

Glue your card solar panels onto each end of the craft stick with the unfolded side onto the stick. If you wish to hang your telescope just tie some fishing line or string to the craft stick and let it orbit!

Flying saucers

What you need
- Two paper plates the same size
- Strong glue
- Felt pens and/or stickers

What you do
Carefully decorate the backs of the plates, making sure not to squash them too much. Also, try not to make them unbalanced with too many stickers in one place.

Glue round the inside edge of both plates and press them firmly together. Keep pressing round until you are sure they won't come apart. Leave them to dry completely.

The finished flying saucers can be thrown like frisbees, although they may not be as efficient!

Games

Use a selection of these space-related games during Lunar landing.

Space race

There are several different relay races you could run – if you have enough room, why not combine them into one giant race!

Planet and spoon: use an oversized 'planet' (eg, a small sponge ball) – the size of the spoon will determine how difficult this race is. You could paint your 'planet' to make it planet-y.

Rings of Saturn: set out a course of hoops which the children have to pass through.

Asteroid belt: create an obstacle course, giving each section a space name, eg 'wormhole' (play tunnel), 'force field' (cargo net) and 'gravity pull' (ball pit).

Space walk: give each team a pair of oversized trousers, filled with balloons. Each child has to put on the trousers and try to run while wearing them! (Make sure you take into account health and safety issues.)

Wormhole: each child has to, in turn, tear a hole in the centre of a sheet of newspaper and pass through it. If they tear the paper by mistake, they start again with a new piece.

Asteroids

What you need
- Space marked out as shown (see page 90)
- One or more large sponge balls (asteroids)

What you do
Divide the players into two teams and position them as shown on page 90. The aim of this game is to try and get as many of the opposing team as possible 'out' – ie, in the force field. To start, two players from each team stand inside the force field behind the opposition. All players have to stay in their allotted areas otherwise a free pass is given to the opposing side.

The asteroids are thrown into the main area. The teams attempt to throw the asteroids over the heads of the opposition to their fellow team members behind them. Meanwhile, the other side tries to intercept the balls and prevent them from reaching the force field. The players in the force field try to hit their opponents below the knee. If someone is hit below the knee, he joins his fellow team members in their force field and continues to try to get the other team out. Play for a set time or until one team is 'out'.

Neutral zone

What you need
- Bin liners filled with scrunched-up newspaper or balloons (or just balls of scrunched-up newspaper)
- Masking tape, chalk or other method of marking the playing area

What you do
Before the game, mark two parallel lines down the centre of the playing area. This is the neutral zone and players are not allowed into it. Divide the players into two teams and place the teams either side of the neutral zone. Divide the balloons (or scrunched-up newspaper) equally between the two teams. Over a set time limit, each team has to throw as many balloons (or balls of paper) over the neutral zone into their opponent's sector. When time is up, count how many balloons (or balls of paper) each side has in their sector. The team with the fewest is the winner.

Planet wars

What you need
- Parachute
- Ball (planet)

What you do
Divide the players into two teams and position them around opposite halves of the parachute (you might want to have a leader either side, in between the two teams, to mark out where each team ends). Throw the planet into the middle of the chute. The two teams should attempt to make the planet fly off the parachute and over the heads of their opponents by moving the parachute up and down. When one team is successful, they get a point. Collect the planet and throw it onto the parachute once more. Play for a certain time, or when one team reaches a certain number of points.

Solar system

What you need
- Parachute

What you do
Position the children around the edge of the parachute, holding it at waist height. Walk round the parachute and label the children with the names of planets (Mercury, Venus, Earth, Mars, Mercury, Venus, Earth, Mars, etc – the number of planets you use depends on the number of children you have). Lift the parachute high in the air, and when it reaches its highest position, call out the name of a planet. The children with that name have to run under the parachute to another position at the edge. When you shout 'Solar system', all the children should run under the chute to a different position. You could also play the rule that any children still under the chute when it comes down again are out for one turn.

You can play a variation of this game with a circle of chairs. Give all the players the name of a planet, but have one chair fewer than there are players. One player starts in the centre of the circle and calls out a planet name. Each player with that name has to move to a new chair, but the player in the middle should try to sit on a chair and leave a different player in the middle. When 'Solar system' is called, all the players change places.

Space invaders

What you need
- Disc/foam-ball shooters (or lots of bean bags)
- Empty cans, paper/plastic cups or cardboard tubes, with pictures of different spacecraft stuck on (see template on page 90)

What you do
You can play this game with disc or foam-ball shooters, or with bean bags (call them meteorites!). Before the session, stick the different spacecraft onto the cans/cups/tubes. Stack the spacecraft in pyramids on one side of the room and give the children the shooters or meteorites. Position the players a certain distance from the pyramids and challenge them to knock down as many craft as they can with the shooters or meteorites. Award points for the best aim! You could also award different points for different spacecraft, etc – choose the best method of scoring for your situation.

Astronaut drive

What you need
- Pencils and paper
- Copies of the astronaut diagram from page 91
- Dice

What you do
Place the children in small groups of about four to six. Give a copy of the astronaut diagram to each group and give each child a pencil and a sheet of paper. Each child takes it in turn to throw the dice and draw the part of the astronaut that corresponds to that number. However, you must get the body (number 1) before you can add any other parts! The player to complete their astronaut first is the winner.

Robot fashion show

What you need
- 'Junk' such as cardboard boxes, silver foil, egg boxes, coloured paper
- Sticky tape, masking tape, gaffer tape
- Scissors

What you do
Share out the junk equally between the groups. Challenge the children to build a robot with the junk

they have been given. Set a certain time limit and, once that is up and everyone has finished, parade the robots for all to see. If you wish, you could get an impartial judge to choose the best one.

You could make this challenge a bit more difficult by asking the groups to dress a group member up as a robot. This way, your robots can move about!

Sleeping lions (for Voyage 5)
All but one or two players are 'lions' and lie down on the floor, eyes closed, as if they are sleeping. The remaining one or two players ('hunters') move about the room attempting to encourage the lions to move. The hunters can't touch the lions but may move close to them, tell things to them, jokes, etc. Any lion who moves must stand up and join the hunters.

And if you have a bit more time, space and money…

Rocket launch
What you need
- Resources needed to build a water bottle rocket (websites such as **www.bbc.co.uk/bang/handson/waterbottlerockets.shtml** give you all the details on how to make these)
- Large open space
- Measuring tape

What you do
Give each group the resources needed to build a water bottle rocket, together with materials they can use to decorate it. Make sure each group has a leader. Once each group has finished, take the rockets outside and fire them one by one. Measure how far each one goes – the rocket that travels the furthest is the winner!

Gravity pull
What you need
- Bungee run (available from some Play Associations or inflatable hire companies)

What you do
Bungee runs are giant inflatables where two people compete to run the furthest while tied to a bungee rope. If you have the space and resources to be able to hire these (an internet search will help you find local suppliers), then hold competitions between representatives from each group (different bungee runs have different objectives). Be creative with the way you describe the game – talk in terms of being pulled back by gravity, escaping a planet's gravitational field, etc. This is an ideal game to consider if you are holding a family event as part of *Space Academy*, as it is popular with all ages and requires little skill!

'Tell the story' scripts
Voyage 1 Bible story script
Another planet
A long time ago in the time of the Old Testament, before Jesus came on the earth, there was a very powerful king. He had a very long name – Nebuchadnezzar. King Neb (we could call him) attacked the city of Jerusalem where God's people lived. He took some of them as prisoners to Babylon, his capital city. Babylon seemed like a very strange place to God's people: different clothes, different buildings, different food and different customs. Worst of all, the people of Babylon did not believe in God. They had their own false gods of wood, stone and metal and they worshipped those instead. In fact, everything was so different it must have seemed like… well, like another planet!

At this point ask the children to imagine they are journeying to another planet. Tell them it's a bumpy ride and encourage everyone to lurch from side to side, abruptly. Include flashing lights, music and sound effects. After a short while get everyone to settle down and repeat after you, 'Phew – are we there yet?'

Fit to serve
One day King Neb ordered his highest palace official to choose some young men from God's people to be trained for three years so that they could become court officials. He said 'They must be healthy, handsome, clever, wise, educated, and fit to serve in the royal palace'. The palace official found four people who were all these things.

Invite four children to join you at the front and give them the name tags you've prepared. Read these out and say them with the children a few times so they become familiar with them. (We've chosen the most well-known names even though they are a mix of Hebrew and Babylonian.)

Forbidden food?
King Neb offered Daniel, Shadrach, Meshach and Abednego food from his table, which sounded like a good deal. What could be wrong with eating royal food? Surely that would be the very best there was?

Give the children at the front the play food items or card food and ask everyone else which of these foods they like to eat.

But, do you know what? They didn't want to eat the king's food! *(Tell the children to shake their heads when offered the food.)* Why not?

Loving God

Daniel wanted to show that he still loved God after all the bad things that had happened. He didn't think God had given up on his people and he wanted to do what he knew God had told them. This included only eating the right sort of food. The king's food had probably been used to worship the false gods of Babylon. (Remember, they didn't know about the real God.) And maybe the king's food was food that God's people weren't allowed to eat, like pork. So Daniel, Shadrach, Meshach and Abednego thought it would be safer to become vegetarians.

Vegetables

Give each of your volunteers a vegetable. Ask everyone which of these vegetables they like eating.

Daniel asked the king's chief official, Ashpenaz, if he, Shadrach, Meshach and Abednego could eat just vegetables instead of the king's food. But Ashpenaz was worried he'd get into trouble if he said yes. So Daniel asked the guard if they could have vegetables for the next ten days. He said 'When the ten days are up, compare how we look with the other young men, and decide what to do with us.'

The guard wasn't sure but at last he agreed and at the end of the trial period, can you guess what happened? The Bible says they looked much stronger and healthier than the others, so they were allowed to carry on eating vegetables.

Well educated

Now, if you remember, these men – Daniel, Shadrach, Meshach and Abednego – were chosen to be trained to serve in King Neb's royal court. They had to learn really hard stuff and all about the history of the Babylonians.

Bring out several heavy books that look like hard work to read. Give them to the four children and tell them to get learning.

God really was with them

Then the Bible says a wonderful thing happened. God stepped in and proved he was with them. At the end of the three years King Neb interviewed them and discovered that, of all the men, they were the best. So Daniel, Shadrach, Meshach and Abednego started work at the royal court for King Neb.

But will Daniel, Shadrach, Meshach and Abednego continue to stand firm, when the people around them don't believe in their God? How will they manage now they are trained and have to use their training? Find out tomorrow!

Voyage 2 Bible story script

Another planet

A long time ago in the time of the Old Testament, before Jesus came on the earth, there was a very powerful king. Can you remember his name? Yes, King Nebuchadnezzar, but we'll call him King Neb. One morning, King Neb woke with a start – he'd had such a weird dream that it seemed as if he was on another planet.

In a similar way to yesterday, ask the children to imagine they are journeying to another planet and provide flashing lights, music and sound effects. Everyone lurches from side to side, abruptly, showing that it is a bumpy ride. After a short while get everyone to settle down and repeat after you, 'Phew – that was a really rough dream.'

Worried

Now show or draw the first visual, which is the king's face with a worried look on it.

The king was so worried by the terrible dream that he couldn't get back to sleep again. It was all so real and so weird – what could it mean?

Fill in the word squares to make the word DREAM appear or write it under the face.

Angry

King Neb called in all his counsellors, advisers, magicians and wise men and said, 'I'm worried about a dream I've had and I want to know what it means.' (As an aside: What a very unusual mix of people to make important decisions! It would be very odd if a politician today were to ask a magician for advice. Still, as we're finding out, things were very different in Babylon in those days.)

Anyway, the counsellors, advisers, magicians and wise men said to him, 'Tell us your dream, and we will explain it to you.'

But the king said, 'No! I've made up my mind. If you don't tell me both the dream and its meaning, you will be chopped to pieces and your houses will be torn down. However, if you do tell me both the dream and its meaning, you will be greatly rewarded and highly honoured.'

The counsellors, advisers, magicians and wise men said to him, 'Tell us your dream, and we will explain it to you.'

But the king said, 'No! Tell me the dream, and that will prove that you can interpret it.'

But how could they possibly know that?! The counsellors, advisers, magicians and wise men said, 'No one can do this, apart from the gods, and they don't live among human beings!'

(At this point get another leader to start up a bit of pantomime banter, 'Oh yes they do-ooo!' You reply, 'Oh no they don't!')

When the king heard that his counsellors, advisers, magicians and wise men wouldn't do what he asked, he was furious! *(Draw or reveal the angry face.)*

So the king issued the order to kill all his counsellors, advisers, magicians and wise men. And even though they were not there at the time, the counsellors, advisers, magicians and wise men included Daniel and his friends! *(Reveal the word KILL.)*

The first that Daniel, Shadrach, Meshach and Abednego knew about any of this was when Arioch, the king's official, came to fetch them to be killed!

Daniel asked him, 'Why did the king give such cruel orders?'

Arioch explained what had happened – and Daniel rushed off to the king.

'Give me more time and I'll explain your dream,' he promised.

The king agreed and Daniel went home and told his friends what had happened. Then he said, 'Pray that God will explain this mystery, so that we and the others won't be put to death.'

Surprised
That same night God showed Daniel the answer to the mystery. Wow! 'Take me to the king,' Daniel told Arioch. 'I will tell him the dream.' So he did. The king was amazed. Draw or reveal the surprised face. Daniel got everything exactly right. It was all about a giant statue. *Fill in the word STATUE. Draw each bit of the statue as it is described.*

Happy
'This was the dream,' said Daniel. 'Now I will tell Your Majesty what it means.'

A smile began to grow over the king's face as Daniel explained about him being the head of gold, ruling over the greatest empire of all. Draw or reveal the happy face. Daniel explained that the silver body and arms meant another empire would come after the king and not be as great as his. The bronze waist meant there would be a third empire, which would rule over the whole earth. Finally, there would be a strong fourth empire that would be divided up and weakened like iron and clay would be. During this time a new kingdom would be set up, that would never end. 'The great God is telling Your Majesty what will happen in the future,' said Daniel. *Fill in the word FUTURE.*

(As an aside, if you wish: These empires have come and gone, as Daniel said they would. Christians believe this new kingdom began when Jesus came to earth (a long time after Daniel lived). You'll be finding out more about that in Lunar landing. But, now, back to the story...)

After this, King Neb bowed down and ordered offerings to be made to Daniel. He gave him a high position, saying 'Your God is the greatest of all gods, the Lord over kings.'

So Daniel, Shadrach, Meshach and Abednego were saved from death. But will they be able to stand up to the challenge? What other tests of courage, faith and being different will they have to face? Find out tomorrow!

Voyage 3 Bible story script
Before telling the story, explain that you will need some volunteers to play instruments and some to be flames. Show the children the signals you have decided to use for starting and stopping the music and starting and stopping moving as the flames. Practise them a few times so they know what to do when it comes to that part in the story.

Another planet
A long time ago in the time of the Old Testament, before Jesus came on the earth, there was a very powerful king. You know his name now – King Neb. Today's story is all about Daniel's three friends: Shadrach, Meshach and Abednego. They woke up early one morning and looked out of the window and saw something stunning. It looked like it had come from another planet!

As before, this is the cue for flashing lights, music and sound effects. Everyone lurches from side to side, abruptly. After a short while get everyone to settle down and repeat after you, 'Wow – that's a stunning statue – it's huge.'

Big statue
And it was huge – twenty-seven metres tall and three metres wide, and all made of gold! Well, actually, it would have been covered in gold as there wouldn't have been enough gold in Babylon for it to be solid gold... but still pretty impressive! To give you an idea of how big it was, the Angel of the North (a sculpture in Gateshead) is twenty metres high. *(Show a picture of the Angel of the North, preferably with one that has people in it to give an idea of scale – there are plenty on the internet.)*

Bad news
King Neb gave orders for everyone in the kingdom to come to a ceremony for the statue. The herald announced that when the music played everyone

must bow down and worship the statue or be burnt alive in a blazing furnace. Oh dear! King Neb had not remembered what he'd already learnt! Yesterday we heard that he thought God was the greatest – but now he's telling everyone to worship a statue he's had made himself!

The king's announcement was very bad news for Shadrach, Meshach and Abednego. They were friends of the Lord God of heaven and wanted to do what he said. We've already seen how they stood up for God in Voyage 1 by eating just vegetables. The second of God's Ten Rules (Commandments) said they were not to worship any other gods. So what could they do? I wonder what you would have done.

Invite three volunteers to come out to the front as Shadrach, Meshach and Abednego. Ask your 'musicians' to get ready. Remind them of the signals you agreed at the beginning of Tell the story.

The king signalled to his musicians and said 'Start the music!' Musicians started playing. When they did, all the people bowed down... apart from Shadrach, Meshach and Abednego.

The king signalled again and said, 'Stop the music!'

Now there were some troublemakers in the crowd. They wanted to get Shadrach, Meshach and Abednego into trouble so they reported to the king that these men hadn't bowed down to the statue. 'WHAT!' the king shouted out in anger. 'I'll give you one more chance. If you bow down when the music starts; fine. If not, it's the furnace for you!'

'START THE MUSIC!' he shouted.

Again musicians play and the three volunteers refuse to bow down.

'STOP THE MUSIC!' the king bellowed. 'Do you think there is any god who can save you?' he asked Shadrach, Meshach and Abednego. They replied, 'The God we worship can save us from you and the flaming furnace. But even if he doesn't, we still won't worship your gods and the gold statue'. What an amazing thing to say!

Hot stuff

This made King Neb very angry and his face turned red. He ordered the furnace to be heated up seven times hotter than usual. He told the strongest men from his army to tie up Shadrach, Meshach and Abednego and throw them in. It was so hot that these soldiers got burnt up as they threw the three men in.

Get the children with 'flames' to come out and start waving them about as the fire. Then ask some big children or leaders to push the three into the 'fire' (gently – not too much realism).

The fourth person

Suddenly, the king jumped up. 'What?' he shouted. 'I thought we threw three into the fire. There are four of them now walking around unhurt, and the fourth one looks like a god.'

(*As an aside:* I wonder who that could be. When you get to your Lunar landing groups you'll be thinking about who this fourth person was.)

King Neb called the three men out of the blazing fire and everyone crowded around them. They were not burnt, their hair wasn't scorched, and their clothes didn't even smell of smoke!

Wow! King Neb told everyone to praise the God of Shadrach, Meshach and Abednego. He realised that this God was the greatest. He'd never known a god who could rescue like this.

So, once again Shadrach, Meshach and Abednego are rescued from death. But what other strange goings-on will there be in Babylon? Find out tomorrow!

Voyage 4 Bible story script

Before telling the story, explain that you will need the children to take part later. Tell them they will need to make noises and pretend to express panic and fear, starting off quietly and getting louder and louder. Remind the children of the stop/start signals you decided on yesterday and say that you'll be using them again today. NB 'Another planet' comes later in the story today.

Setting the scene

We've jumped to many years later from yesterday's story, but things are much the same for Daniel. He's still living in Babylon, he's still working for the king and he's still worshipping God. But there's a new king in Babylon. He's called Belshazzar – we'll call him Bel.

One evening, Bel had... a small get-together with his friends? No. A little party for his neighbours? No. He had an ENORMOUS banquet! Guess how many people he invited? One thousand! Imagine that. What a lot of food that would be! *Ask the children to come up with some suggestions of what they might have eaten.*

Not a good idea

The party was in full swing when King Bel had an idea. He thought it was a great idea – but actually it wasn't. He remembered that ages ago some special gold and silver cups had been taken from the Temple in Jerusalem, the special building where people had worshipped God. He ordered his servants to get them, and everyone at the banquet started drinking from them. Not only did they drink out of God's special cups but they also started to praise their gods – not the real God – but the ones made of gold, silver, wood and stone.

Another planet
Suddenly, something very weird and scary happened. It was just the sort of thing that could have come from another planet…

Cue for flashing lights, music and sound effects. Everyone lurches from side to side, abruptly. After a short while get everyone to settle down and repeat after you, 'Wow – that's weird and scary!'

The writing on the wall
A human hand appeared, on its own, with no person attached! The fingers started writing words on the wall. King Bel saw the hand as it was writing and he was petrified. The Bible says, 'He was so frightened that his face turned pale, his knees started shaking, and his legs became weak.' (I'm not surprised – it would have been terrifying!)

If you are using the wax idea, you could try painting a thin line through the middle of the wax so that something appears, but hopefully not clear enough to read, if you have made the wax letters really large.

Here we go again
Bel called for his magicians, advisors and wise men. He told them, 'If any of you can read the writing and tell me what it means, I'll make you the third most powerful man in my kingdom and you will wear royal robes and a gold chain.' Do you think they could? Of course not! Now King Bel was more afraid than ever before, and the Bible says 'his face turned white as a ghost'! No one knew what to do… so they started to panic! Quietly at first, until the noise got louder and louder.

Encourage the children to make noises to express panic and fear that start off quietly and get louder and louder. Be ready to cover your ears and give the children a signal when you want them to stop.

Daniel to the rescue
Finally the queen came in, having heard all the noise. Guess who she told Bel about? Yes, Daniel. By now he was probably about 80, which is why he didn't come with the rest of the advisors. She told Bel that Daniel was wise, intelligent and could explain dreams and riddles and solve difficult problems. So the king sent for him.

'Now then, if you can read this writing and tell me what it means, you will become the third most powerful man in my kingdom. You will wear royal purple robes and have a gold chain around your neck', he promised Daniel.

But Daniel refused Bel's gifts.

'Your Majesty, I will read the writing and tell you what it means. God made your father, King Neb, very great and powerful. He was so great that people of all nations were afraid of him and trembled,' Daniel said. 'But he became proud and stubborn and was removed from his royal throne and driven away from human society. He lived outside like an animal until he came to his senses and admitted that God rules all kingdoms and chooses their kings,' he continued.

'King Bel, you knew all this, but still refused to honour God. Instead, you turned against him. You used his special cups and you praised your gods made of gold, silver, wood and stone. That's why God sent the hand to write the words on the wall.'

The words on the wall
Get your paint and get ready to paint over the words to reveal them one by one as you explain them.

Daniel then explained the message on the wall as follows:

Numbered: Your days are numbered, and you won't be king any more.

Weighed: (bit tricky this one). God says you don't weigh up to his standards and you don't do what he wants.

Divided: Your kingdom will be divided and given to the Medes and Persians. (These were two big countries to the north of Babylon that had a lot of power.)

And it all happened that very night.

The army of the Medes and Persians arrived.

Darius the Mede became king.

Belshazzar had fallen short of what it takes to be king.

Belshazzar was king no more. (Pause)

What a serious end to the party! I wonder what this new king will be like? Will his kingdom accept Daniel's God or not? Find out tomorrow!

Voyage 5 Bible story script

Another planet
As we found out at the end of yesterday's story, King Bel was no longer king. Darius became king instead. He wasn't from Babylon and he didn't know about God either.

Daniel was so good that even his **enemies** couldn't see anything he did wrong. In fact, you would almost think he had come from another planet.

This is the cue for flashing lights, music and sound effects. Everyone lurches from side to side, abruptly, and then settles down as they repeat after you, 'Wow how come he's so good?'

How could it be? It was because **Daniel** loved God so much. He always wanted to do things right and do his best for God. **King** Darius promoted him to be the top man in Babylon. But the people **Daniel** worked with were jealous of him. They didn't like him getting all the best jobs and, without **Daniel** doing anything against them, they became his **enemies**. They wanted to catch him out, and they came up with a horrible **plan**.

We need to talk
Explain to the children that they need to find a 'Talk partner'. Many of them will know what this is from school. Children talk to the person next to them, but make sure no one is left out; team can also join in.

Turn to your talk partner and tell them your favourite food. This time, you aren't allowed to speak so you have to use signs to tell them your favourite TV programme. Now tell them your favourite game, but you can't speak or use your hands! Getting hard isn't it? Trying to tell someone something without talking or signing is really difficult. OK, you can talk again. Tell your talk partner about your last two favourite things if they didn't get them.

We need to talk, especially to our friends. It's not easy when someone tells you that you are not allowed to talk to your friend. That's what happened to **Daniel** (hooray – remind the children about the sound effects if they forget to cheer here). As you know, **Daniel** was great friends with God and talked to him often, and this is what his **enemies** picked on with their **plan**.

The Sneaky Plan
'We'll have to get him somehow,' his **enemies** schemed. 'Not to do with his work – **Daniel** is too good. Not to do with telling the truth – he always does.' They spied on Daniel and realised the only way was to find something to do with his God. Finally, his **enemies** came up with a sneaky **plan**. They went to the **king** and told him how wonderful he was, etc, etc, and that they had all agreed that he should bring in a new law that no one should request anything from any god or man for 30 days, except from him, the **king**. **King** Darius. Anyone who disobeyed the new law was to be thrown into a pit filled with **lions** (roar!). A very clever **plan** – and the **king** liked it!

Got him
The **king** signed the order for the plan to be put into action. When **Daniel** found out about the new law, he went home, and as usual he knelt down to talk to God in prayer. The Bible says **Daniel** did this three times a day. Of course, the **enemies** were watching out for this: their **plan** was working; they could almost hear the **lions**. They went to the **king** and told him that **Daniel** was still praying to his God. Now this wasn't what the **king** had wanted at all! The **king** was upset and tried all day to work out how to get round the law, but he couldn't – it had to be. So **Daniel** was arrested and thrown into the pit of **lions**. The **king** said to **Daniel**, 'You have been faithful to your God, and I pray that he will rescue you.'

A stone was rolled over the pit of **lions**, and it was stamped with a seal. The **king** went home – and didn't sleep a wink.

The angel and the lions
At daybreak the **king** got up and ran to the pit. He shouted, 'Was your God able to save you from the **lions**?'

Did **Daniel** respond? Yes! He said, 'God sent an angel to keep the **lions** from eating me.'

The **king** was so relieved. He gave orders for **Daniel** to be taken out of the pit. Cover your ears for the next bit if you are squeamish! The **king** ordered the **enemies** to be thrown into the pit. The **lions** pounced on them before they reached the bottom.

After that, the **king** gave another command that everyone in his kingdom was to worship and honour the God of **Daniel**.

Drama
The Final Frontier

Summary
The drama is set on board a Starship, named after the club/school/town that it is being performed in. Minimal scenery is needed, but 'transporter circles' on the floor on one side of the stage would be helpful and some kind of console, and a large computer in one corner. The cast will need to envisage a 'screen' just off the front of centre stage above the children's heads. Each day the crew try to complete their mission, coming across all sorts of obstacles on the way, and discovering how Mission Command helps them through. A piece of *Star Trek/Star Wars* type music to start and finish, and good sound effects, will make a real difference. This drama is a bit of light relief rather than in-depth teaching. A bit of over-acting or hamming-up the space-i-ness will all add to the fun!

Cast
- **Captain Kim** – male or female. A bit posh and a bit dim, but comes through in the end. Wears a cap or epaulettes to denote rank.
- **Odor** – the baddie. A take-off of the famous Jedi Knight from Star Wars. Needs to be short (preferably on knees), wearing a long gown and have a green head with big ears (possibly made out of a swimming hat).
- **Holly Buddy** – the hologram. Frightened by everything (apart from in Episode Three), wearing shimmery silver clothing.
- **Spot** – logical Vulcanesque-type character. Pointy ears if possible!
- **Prism** – The ship's engineer. Could be human or an alien with a swimming hat with a design painted on the forehead.
- **Cook** – The ship's French cook.
- **Computer** – a head in a cut-out cardboard box, or on a screen. Bit of a cockney, no respect at all for the Captain or crew. This character only appears on board the ship so could double up with other parts.
- **Mission Command** – voice-over.
- **Darth Paul** and **Darth Brenda** – need Darth Vader-style masks.

Episode 1
Today, the crew learn of their instructions from Mission Command.

Script

Captain Kim (*Voice offstage.*): Captain's Log, star date 4567.89, on board the Starship (insert name of church or club). Today we start our space journey, to infinity and beyond! I say, it's dark out there: dark, dark, dark. In fact it's a whole load of black, apart from those white shiny things, of course.

(*Captain Kim walks on stage and presses a few keys on a console, pretending to look at a large screen in front of him/her.*)

Captain Kim: Good morning, computer. I say, old chap, would you mind awfully asking the crew to meet me here on the poop deck for our mission briefing?

Computer: (*Shouting.*) Oi, crew! Get up 'ere! Captain Kim wants ya to get up on the poop!

(*Crew assemble.*)

Captain Kim: Good morning, crew. Welcome Holly Buddy the hologram. I'm glad that they uploaded you successfully. Spot, my second in command – good to have you on board. Prism, the engineer – I've heard a lot about your work, and Cook (*slightly dubiously*) – I've heard a lot about your work too!

Everyone: Good morning, Captain.

Captain Kim: Today is an important day for the crew of the Starship (*Name*). We receive our instructions from Mission Command. Don't know about you, Spot, but I'm a bit excited. You know, got that tingly churning feeling in my tum tum.

Spot: It is logical to feel excited, Captain. It's a great honour to serve Mission Command. I too have a strange sensation in my stomach, but I thought it was the result of Cook's cooking.

Cook: But, of course, my cooking is truly sensational.

Prism: (*Aside.*) Hmm… sensational if you're a pig who hasn't eaten for three weeks and has had their taste buds ripped out!

Cook: I 'eard that, you little bald-headed alien you! (*Tries to hit him over the head with a wooden spoon.*)

Captain Kim: Now, I say, chaps! Order, order! (*The crew calm down and stand in line.*) As I was saying, today is a very important day. Computer, can you get Mission Command on the screen, please?

Computer: I'll see what I can do, matey (hissing, crackling and interference noises). Oh dear, oh dear! Not a very good signal. (*He holds his phone in*

PHOTOCOPIABLE PAGE

the air trying to get a signal and ends up standing in a really odd position.) That's the best I can get guvs. (*The crew all stare at the screen.*)

Mission Command: (*With crackling and hissing noises.*) This is Mission Command. Starship (*Name*), are you receiving us?

Captain Kim: This is Captain Kim from the Starship (*Name*). Do you have our mission instructions?

Mission Command: (*Lots of cracking and disturbance, so that some of the syllables are not heard.*) Now listen carefully. We have reason to believe that our transmissions are being intercepted by our arch enemy, Odor, so I will say this only once. Your mission is to spread the good news of Mission Command as you travel the ...nets of ...ta ...rant, and live life in a way that represents the ...ness, ...ness, ...sity, ...esty and ...cy of Mission Command.

Captain Kim: Er, didn't quite get that, Mission Command. Your message kept coming and going.

Mission Command: Yes, you will be coming and going. In fact, you will be going where no man has gone before. Good luck, and may the force be with you.

Captain Kim: Mission Command? Mission Command? Can you hear me Mission Command?

Spot: As there is no response, Captain, it would be logical to assume that they can no longer hear you.

Captain Kim: Computer, can you get them back?

Computer: No chance. Looks like one of them satellites has shifted or somefink.

Holly Buddy: So what are our instructions, Captain?

Captain Kim: Er... um...

Cook: Oh, it's quite straightforward really. We have to travel the nets of the ta rant, spreading ness, ness, city, esty and see!

Captain Kim: Yes, indeed. (*Trying to put a brave face on it.*) Spreading ness, ness, city, esty and see!

(*They all look at him/her blankly.*)

Prism: Well it's an instruction Kim, but not as we know it!

Captain Kim: Indeed! Spot, you speak 423 languages. Can you translate?

Spot: No, despite the fact that I am now fluent in 424 languages (I learnt Zingyping last week), that sentence is untranslatable. The logical conclusion is that in order to outwit the baddie, Odor, Mission Command has encrypted the message. All we have to do is work out the code

Captain Kim: I say, Spot, I think you might be right. Come on chaps, thinking caps on!

(*They all adopt deep thinking positions. Odor appears at the side or back of the audience.*)

Odor: (*Evil laugh.*) Planning to spoil the mission of the Starship (*Name*) am I. Starting to work it is, by disrupting the signal from Mission Command. Ensured have I that they will never work out that they need to travel the planets of the Delta Quadrant spreading goodness, kindness, generosity, honesty and mercy.

Cook: I've got it!

Everyone: (*Looking expectant.*) What?

Cook: Oh, no – forgotten it now.

(*They all go back to thinking.*)

Prism: I know!

Everyone: (*Looking expectant.*) What?

Prism: Oh no – it won't work.

(*They all go back to thinking.*)

Mission Command: This is Mission Command. Come in Captain Kim and the crew of the Starship (*Name*). Can you hear me?

Captain Kim: Loud and clear, Mission Command.

Mission Command: We have reason to believe that our message was interrupted by the evil Odor, so we are sending it again. Are you ready?

Everyone: Yes.

Mission Command: Your mission is to travel the planets of the Delta Quadrant spreading the good news of Mission Command with goodness, kindness, generosity, honesty and mercy. May the force be with you!

Prism: Ah, so it wasn't ness, ness, city, esty and see after all! Shame, really. I quite fancied going to Ta Rant, wherever that is!

Captain Kim: Computer, set our coordinates for the Delta Quadrant, warp factor 4. We're off to start our mission.

(*They all move as if the ship has got started.*)

Captain Kim: I say, Cook, I don't suppose there's a chance of a cup of tea is there?

Cook: I'll go and put the kettle on.

(*They all follow Cook out.*)

Prism: It won't suit you.

Holly: What?

Prism: The kettle, if she puts it on...

THE ENGINE ROOM — CAPTAIN'S LOG 5

79

Episode 2

In this episode, the crew land on a mysterious planet, meet a mysterious alien and learn that Mission Command is looking after them.

Props
- Big wobbly jelly on a plate that can be moved by a piece of string
- Spot's space tech hardware
- Emergency kit containing squirty cream and spoons

Script

Captain Kim (*Voice offstage.*): Captain's Log, star date 3.1472. Following our instructions from Mission Command, we have arrived at the Delta Quadrant and are currently in orbit around the planet known to its inhabitants as (*Makes and odd and amusing noise.*) The crew is assembling a landing party.

(*The crew, apart from Spot, come on in party hats with streamers doing the Conga.*)

Captain Kim: I say chaps, what on earth are you doing?

Cook: You said we should assemble a landing party. No sausage rolls I'm afraid, Captain, but this was the best we could do at short notice!

Captain: Not that sort of party! A landing party lands on the planet, looks at things, interferes a bit and then escapes to the ship in the nick of time.

(*They all look at each other and make excuses why they can't go. I've got some very important door swishing to attend to; I'm allergic to planets; My knees aren't good for landing, etc. Spot comes on wearing loads of space tech hardware.*)

Spot: Reporting for duty, Captain. I am ready for the landing party. I have got my night-vision binoculars, day-vision binoculars, and sun visor; I have got my sonic screwdriver, sonic secateurs and my sonic handkerchief; I have also got some sandwiches, a spare bottle of water and some sun cream; my phaser is set to stun and my phone is on vibrate so as not to disturb any aliens when we get there.

Captain Kim: Er great, thanks Spot. So come on everyone – to the transporter!

(*They all move to a side of the stage, stand on a set of circles and wiggle to a buzzing noise.*)

Captain: Stop! (*They all stop wiggling.*) I forgot the special emergency kit issued by Mission Command. (*Captain rushes off to get it whilst the rest wait. When he or she returns with the kit, they all wiggle again until they 'land' on the planet, look around them and gingerly start to walk around.*)

Holly: (*Moving stage left where there is a jelly on a table*) (*Scared.*) Captain! Captain! What's this?

Cook: Well, in my expert opinion, honed in the finest restaurants of Paris, it's a jelly.

Holly: No, it's not. It's an alien – we're all doomed!

Captain Kim: Gosh, how exciting! Do you think it's alive?

(*The jelly moves because Odor is pulling a piece of string attached to the plate it is on. The children can see this but the crew can't.*)

Prism: It moved, so it's life, Kim, but not as we know it.

Spot: If we have indeed discovered an alien life form, then the next logical step is to make contact with it.

Captain Kim: Spot on Spot. (*Turning to jelly, saluting and speaking very slowly and loudly.*) My name is Captain Kim, from the Starship (*Name*). We come in peace with messages from Mission Command. Take us to your leader.

(*The jelly wobbles.*)

Cook: Well it looks like it is wobbling in this direction. Quick, let's go!

(*They exit stage left away from Odor, who enters stage right.*)

Odor: (*Evil laugh.*) Fallen for my wicked jelly trap have Captain Kim and his crew. Now waste their time they will wandering around this planet looking for jelly and won't have time to spread the good news of Mission Command. Here they come. Hiding am I!

(*Odor hides.*)

Captain Kim: Well, this looks just like the place where we started. Ah, but there's another alien over here. Perhaps it can show us the way.

Spot: The ground is the same, the setting is the same, that (*insert object*) is the same and the alien looks remarkably similar to the first one we met. It would therefore be logical to assume that this is the place where we started.

Cook: But it cannot be. The first place didn't have this bad smell.

Prism: Yes, now you come to mention it, it is a bit whiffy.

Holly: A bit whiffy? It's horrendous. Even I can smell it and I am a hologram!

Spot: There's only one person who smells like that and that's our dastardly enemy, the evil Odor!

PHOTOCOPIABLE PAGE

Captain Kim: Oh I say, he's not here, is he?

(*Encourage the children to shout, 'He's behind you!' Choreograph some 'behind you' and 'chase' moves that culminate in Odor's face being pushed in the jelly, which Cook is holding.*)

Captain Kim: Quick! Run to the transporter!

(*They run to their circles and wiggle until back on ship.*)

Computer: Oh, back so soon. You've spoiled my nap.

Holly: Phew! That was a bit too close for comfort... what's up Cook?

Cook: (*Crying.*) Oh, the poor alien. Look, it's been crushed!

Prism: (*Sticking his finger in it and licking it.*) It's OK cook – it's only a jelly after all.

Captain Kim: That's as maybe, but it did a very convincing impression of an alien! There were a couple of close shaves there. Just as well we had our emergency kit from Mission Command.

Spot: But Captain, I had all the kit that we needed. What could have possibly been in our emergency kit from Mission Command that we needed?

(*They open the kit to find squirty cream and spoons.*)

Prism: Looks like we can have a landing party after all.

(*They dig in.*)

Episode 3
In today's episode, Holly Buddy comes to the rescue, with the help of Mission Command.

Prop
- Marshmallows

Script
Captain Kim (*Voice offstage.*): Captain's Log, star date 2468. All is well on the Starship (*Name*) as we start another day on our mission to spread the good news of Mission Command with goodness, kindness, generosity, honesty and mercy. Today we are visiting the unusual planet of 'Ware ah ya', where all the inhabitants are invisible.

Captain Kim: (*Entering stage right.*) Where is everyone?

Computer: Well, Spot's playing 3D chess with himself, Prism is tinkering with the ship's engine, Cook is er... cooking (if you can call it that!) and Holly Buddy the hologram... well her battery was low, so she's recharging.

Captain Kim: I say, that's a bit off – we've got a busy day today. Tell them I want them to be at the transporter deck right away.

Computer: Oi, you lot! You'd better get a wriggle on. The Captain's in a right mood!

(*Captain glares at the computer as everyone, apart from Holly, enters and stands by their transporter circle.*)

Captain Kim: Good morning, crew. Bit of a jolly jape today. We're going to a planet where all the inhabitants are invisible, so keep your wits about you, and don't tread on anyone!

(*They all wiggle as they transport and arrive on the planet.*)

Voice-over: (*In a big booming voice.*) People of 'Ware ah ya'. It is time.

Prism: Time? Time for what?

Cook: I don't know, but I think I can hear people coming this way!

Spot: Quick, hide!

(*They all hide behind something and mime watching a whole lot of people moving from stage left to stage right, and back again.*)

Cook: Oooh, that was scary, but I think they've gone now.

Spot: It would be logical to follow them to find out what is happening.

Captain Kim: Hmm... I'm not so sure. Let's split up and explore whilst they appear to be busy.

(*They all exit stage left. Prism enters stage left and starts looking round. Odor creeps in behind him.*)

Odor: (*In stage whisper to audience.*) Putting my wicked plan into action am I and stopping these people spreading the good news of Mission Command. (*He hides and says to Prism in a disguised voice.*) It's nice here, isn't it?

Prism: Who said that?

Odor: Oh, no one in particular – just your conscience. Look around you, Prism. What do you see? Have a marshmallow. (*Prism helps himself.*) Isn't it so much better than home?

Prism: Well, I suppose so, but I love my life on board the Starship (*Name*).

Odor: Yes Prism, it's a life, but not as we know it. On this planet we have everything we need and more. Come, sit down, take a rest, and enjoy the good life.

(*Prism settles down and falls asleep. Cook and Spot enter, ignoring Prism. Odor sneaks up behind them and sticks his fingers in their backs, like guns.*)

Odor: (*In a disguised voice.*) Hands up! You are under arrest. You have infringed our planet's laws by being visible in public. Walk this way. (*He pushes them over to stage right, making sure they cannot see him at all.*) I am tying your hands to this invisible tree, with invisible rope. Do not try to get away.

Cook and **Spot**: (*Scared.*) No, of course not. We won't budge a centimetre.

Odor: (*Stage whisper to audience.*) Now, all I've got to do is that Captain find, and then, persuaded all of them have I, not to bother with their stupid mission from Mission Command.

(*Captain enters. Odor hides.*)

Captain Kim: Oh I say, bit of a nasty niff round here. If I didn't know better I would say that desperate baddie Odor had been hanging round here.

(*Odor creeps up behind Captain, does a 'He's behind you' thing with the children, until the two of them eventually bump into each other.*)

Captain Kim: Ah, so it is you, Odor!

Odor: Yes, it is I, Odor, one of the most brilliantly evil minds in the universe. Odor, fiend above all fiends, destroyer of all that is good, baddest of the bad am I.

Captain Kim: (*Scared.*) Ah well, I am er… Captain K-kim, erm on a Mission from Mission Command, spreading ness, ness, city, esty and see.

Odor: (*Scornfully.*) ness, ness, city, esty and see?

Captain Kim: Yes, I mean, no, I mean. Oh!

Odor: Thinking am I Captain, that you are not good at what you do. Mission Command is foolish to be trusting you. Rubbish you are.

Captain Kim: No, I mean, yes, I mean. Oh!

Odor: Pointless your mission is. Give it up, Captain, give it up.

Captain Kim: Yes, I mean no, I mean, yeah maybe you're right.

(*Captain slumps down on to the floor. As Odor starts to do a victory dance, Holly Buddy bounces onto the stage.*)

Holly: (*Full of energy and life, as she bounces around stretching, she narrowly misses hitting Odor several times.*) Sorry I'm late everyone. Had to get my battery charged, but I'm here now, so what's going on? Captain, what's wrong?

Captain Kim: Oh hello, Holly. It's OK, you don't need to call me Captain anymore. I've given up our mission; it was a waste of time thinking I could do it anyway.

Cook: Ah, Holly come and untie us. We've been tied to this invisible tree with invisible rope.

(*Prism wakes up.*)

Prism: Stop shouting, guys. Chill, enjoy, eat another marshmallow. (*He tries to go back to sleep.*)

Holly: (*In a crowd-rousing, inspiring voice.*) This is ridiculous! Have you all forgotten what we are supposed to be doing? Our mission is really important and yet here you are moping, sleeping and pretending to be tied to a tree!

Spot: We're not pretending – we really are tied with invisible rope. (*Realises that hands are free.*) Ah, well – it was a logical conclusion on a planet of invisible people that they would have invisible rope!

Holly: No, it was not logical, Spot, and neither is it logical, Captain, to give up. Who on earth told you not to carry on with our important mission?

Captain Kim: (*Embarrassed.*) Well, it was Odor.

Holly: And you believed that stinking wretch of a villain? Mission Command believes in you, so I believe in you. Come on! Help me revive Prism from his marshmallow-induced stupor, and let's get out of here.

(*They all grab Prism, stand on their transporter circles and wiggle.*)

Computer: (*Sarcastically.*) Welcome back crew. Cor blimey am I glad to see you. (*Embarrassed.*) Er… what wiv one fing and another I sorta managed to get your plugs mixed up, Holly. It turns out I plugged you into the Mission Command mainframe instead of the battery recharger. Are you OK?

Captain Kim: She's never been better, have you Holly?

Holly: No, but I am a bit peckish now. Any chance of a bite to eat, Cook?

(*They all follow Cook off, Prism holding his tummy and groaning. Odor pops up at the side.*)

Odor: Hmm… foiled am I this time, but back I will be!

Episode 4

In this episode, Mission Command helps the crew defeat Odor.

Prop
● Remote-control-style black box

Script
Captain Kim: (*Voice offstage.*) Captain's Log, star date 369.963. Following our various adventures around the planets of the Delta Quadrant, we are journeying towards the planet Ping, sister planet to the completely uninhabitable planet of Pong.

(*There is an almighty creaking, crashing sound.*)

PHOTOCOPIABLE PAGE

THE ENGINE ROOM

Captain Kim: (*Running on to the stage.*) Computer, Computer! What's happening? The ship has ground to a halt.

Computer: You're not wrong there, Captain.

(*Prism, Cook, Holly and Spot come running on.*)

Prism: Captain, Captain! The ship has run aground!

Spot: That is not a logical conclusion; this ship is in space, a gravityless void, so by definition it cannot run aground.

Holly: So, what's that out of the window?

(*They all stare at the screen in horror.*)

Cook: It looks like a massive great big rock to me.

Prism: (*Rubbing it in.*) So which bit of the gravityless void has got dirty great big bits of rock in, Spot?

Spot: Well, obviously that bit, but there is still no evidence that that is actually ground.

Prism: Well...

Captain Kim: (*Interrupting.*) I say chaps, calm down! I'm sure that we are agreed that it doesn't actually matter how we describe it. What really matters is what we are going to do about it.

(*While this is going on, Odor has sneaked on to the back of the stage.*)

Odor: Right you are, Captain Kim. The big question is what you are going to do about it.

(*They all step back in horror.*)

Everyone: Odor!

Odor: Yes, it is I, Odor, one of the most brilliantly evil minds in the universe. Odor, fiend above all fiends, destroyer of all that is good, baddest of the bad...

Captain Kim: Yes, yes, we did all that yesterday. Now what on earth are you doing on board my ship?

Odor: Come to watch how you deal with my ultimate weapon, have I. Calling it the very big, size-of-a-planet bomb am I!

(*Everyone looks back at the screen in horror.*)

Prism: You mean that is a bomb?

Odor: Exactly, and you have exactly 3.5 minutes before exploding it is, taking your precious ship and everyone in it! (*He gets out a big stopwatch and looks at it. Everyone runs around screaming and bumping into each other.*)

Captain Kim: I say, chaps, this is not helping. We've got to come up with a plan.

(*They all strike a thinking pose.*)

Captain Kim: Anything?

Holly: We could run around screaming.

Prism: We've tried that!

Cook: I could make us all a nice cup of tea.

Spot: I estimate that by the time the kettle has boiled, we will all have gone ... boom!

Odor: (*Evil laugh.*) Where's your precious Mission Command now, then? Huh? (*Starts throwing a small black box up and down.*) Of course, if the remote control you were having, you could stop it!

Holly: Quick, he's got the remote control!

Captain Kim: Get him!

(*Keystone-Kops-style chase scene around the room. Eventually everyone arrives back on stage, and the Captain has the black box. Odor has his back to the screen.*)

Captain Kim: Aha, now you're not so clever! We have the remote control, and we can stop your silly 'very big, size-of-a-planet bomb'!

Odor: (*Evil laugh.*) Thinking I am that stupid, are you? The remote control needs a code to activate it, and knowing the code only is I. Foiled again are you, Captain Kim.

Computer: (*Looking at the screen.*) Captain, Captain! There's a message coming in from Mission Command.

Captain Kim: Not now, Computer. I'm a little bit busy right now.

Computer: But Captain, it's really important.

Captain Kim: OK. Well put it up on the screen... it's just a set of numbers.

Spot: Yes, Captain, but one can assume that it is not just any set of numbers! It's the deactivation code!

Odor: (*Turning round to look at the screen.*) Nooooo! (*He falls to his knees.*)

Cook: Quick! Enter it into the remote control.

Captain Kim; (*As he is entering the numbers.*) 7,2,3,9 What's that last number?

Prism: It's a five Captain, but not as we know it!

Captain Kim: Five. That's it! Look it's flashing.

(*They all do a stage shift.*)

Spot: It would seem logical to conclude that the 'very big, size-of-a-planet bomb' has dropped off the front of our ship.

(*Everyone cheers.*)

Cook: But what about old smelly here? What are we going to do with him?

Prism: Maybe we should give him a taste of his own medicine!

Holly: Yes, he frightened the life out of me; he obviously doesn't appreciate my nerves!

CAPTAIN'S LOG 5

Captain Kim: No, our mission has been to spread the good news of Mission Command with goodness, kindness, generosity, honesty and MERCY.

Spot: Indeed, but we can't just leave him. The stink is making me feel ill!

Computer: Captain, there's another message coming in from Mission Command… It says he is their problem, not ours.

Captain Kim: Well in that case we'll send him to Mission Command.

(They put him on a transporter circle, he wiggles and disappears.)

Prism: Now, Cook. Did you mention a cup of tea?

Cook: I'll go and put the kettle on.

Captain Kim: I say, what a splendid idea – I am rather parched.

(They all exit discussing the various merits of tea in space.)

Episode 5

In this last episode, the crew discover that asking Mission Command for help can really make a difference.

Props
- large cardboard boxes
- heavy breathing sound effect

Script

Captain Kim: (*Voice offstage.*) Captain's Log, star date 999911999. The crew of the Starship (*Name*) have boldly gone where no ship has gone before as we've visited the planets of the Delta Quadrant, spreading the good news of Mission Command with goodness, kindness, generosity, honesty and mercy. Today we visit our last planet, a mysterious metal planet that looks like half of it is missing, and is rumoured to go by the name of 'Not-alive-star'.

(Captain enters.)

Captain: I say, Computer, would you be a jolly good chap and ask the crew to assemble on the transporter deck?

Computer: Oi, you lot, get yourselves up 'ere!

(The crew assemble on stage.)

Captain: Good morning, crew. Our last mission. Now watch yourselves down there. I don't know why but something tells me that 'Not-alive-star' is not a nice place. But our mission is to spread the good news of Mission Command with goodness, kindness, generosity, honesty and mercy, and that is what we are going to do. Phasers on stun and ready to transport!

(They wiggle and land. As they are starting to explore they hear heavy breathing.)

Holly: What's that noise? This is it – we're doomed!

Spot: (*Scanning the area.*) There definitely is some kind of life form on this planet, but the reading is very faint. It would be logical to assume that whoever, or whatever, it is, is hiding deeper within the planet.

Captain: Right, well in that case we really ought to go and find it. Holly, you come with me. Spot, you and Prism go that way, and Cook, you wait here.

(They head off in two different directions leaving Cook despondently behind.)

Cook: That's right, leave me behind, just because I am a cook and not a soldier. I mean, look at this – just a great big pile of boxes. See, nothing here but rubbish. (*Uncovers Darth Paul but doesn't notice. Darth Paul goes to pounce on Cook but hears the others coming so stands still. The others back towards each other across the stage with their phasers in front of them.*)

Spot: The force is getting stronger. It must be around here somewhere.

Holly: I can't see anything: I can just hear that dreadful noise.

(They all bump into each other in the middle of the stage. When they have got over the confusion they notice Darth Paul. Holly faints and is caught by Prism.)

Captain: I say! Looks like we've found the big bad breathy thing. He was here all along. Er…(*Talking loudly and slowly.*) Hello, my name is Captain Kim from the Starship (*Name*). What's your name?

Darth Brenda: (*Coming on from the side.*) I'll tell you what his name is. It's 'Mr I'd rather hide in cardboard boxes than help my wife with the washing up'. (*Stands with arms folded glaring at Darth Paul.*)

Prism: (*Aside stage whisper.*) Well, he's got a wife, but not as we know it!

Darth Brenda: I heard that!

Darth Paul: My name is Darth Paul and I have been left here by the Empire to guard the 'Not-alive-star' with my wife Darth Brenda.

Captain: Well, jolly good to meet you Darth Paul, Darth Brenda.

Darth Paul: Captain – come over to the dark side.

Prism: Watch out, Captain, he is trying to make you into a baddie.

PHOTOCOPIABLE PAGE

Darth: No I'm not. I mean, come over here. I can't see you properly when you stand in the light like that!

Prism: Awkward!

Darth Brenda: He's not bad at all. He's a lovely, fluffy bunny-wunny!

(*They rub noses and snuggle up while the others stick their fingers down their throats, etc.*)

Spot: But that is not logical. History tells us that all the Darths are evil cape-wearing, light sabre-carrying, wheezing giants who can kill you by just doing this.

(*He tries squeezing his fingers together, like Darth Vader did.*)

Darth Paul: Oh yeah, I used to be very bad. I could do the evil laugh and everything, but then I met someone from Mission Command and they showed me a different way. Now we live for ness, ness, city, esty and see.

Captain: I think you'll find that's (*getting the children to join in*) goodness, kindness, generosity, honesty and mercy.

Darth Paul and Darth Brenda: (*Looking at each other in wonder.*) Oh yes, that makes a lot more sense.

Cook: So what's with the heavy breathing and the... (*She poses in Darth's pounce pose.*)

Holly: Yes, you scared the life out of me!

Prism: Yes, but let's face it – that's not difficult!

Darth Paul: Well, I thought you lot were thieves. And the breathing... well I think it's blocked sinuses. Give me right jip they do.

Darth Brenda: Oh yes, it keeps us up at night, and you should hear the snoring.

Captain: Have you thought about getting help from Mission Command?

Darth: No. Do you think that would really work?

Captain: Well, it's worth a try.

Darth Paul: But how?

Spot: It's simple. Just call him on your telecommunications device.

(*Darth Paul uses his phone.*)

Darth Paul: Hello, is that Mission Command? ...Yes, it's nice to speak to you too... Yes, it was a bit of a shock to receive visitors after all this time, but they seem quite nice... OK, I'll tell them that... Yes, well I was just wondering if you could do something about the heavy breathing... yes, and my snoring keeps Darth Brenda up at night... Really? Well that's a brilliant idea. I'll try it. (*He takes off his mask.*) Ah yes, I can breathe, I can breathe! And you think it will work for Darth Brenda too? (*He encourages Darth Brenda to take her mask off too.*) Oh thank you so much Mission Command... Yes OK, I won't forget to call again soon... Bye, and thank you.

Captain: Well, you look fantastic Darth Paul, Darth Brenda. What a difference Mission Command has made.

Darth Paul: Yes, oh and he gave me a message for you. He said, 'Well done for completing your mission. You have done well Starship (*Name*) in spreading the good news of Mission Command with (*everyone joins in*) goodness, kindness, generosity, honesty and mercy.'

Space Academy theme song — God's way

Driving and confident ($\quarter = 150$)

Gareth and Steve Hutchinson

1. Da - niel lived God's way, the king was a - mazed, he saw that Da - niel was the best. So far from home he still be - lieved in God; when we're all a - lone, let's learn to trust in God!
2. Da - niel lived God's way, he had to be brave, he showed the mea - ning of the dream. When he faced the king he still be - lieved in God; if we're e - ver scared, let's learn to trust in God!
3. Da - niel lived God's way, the men said, 'Don't pray!', he prayed to God three times a day. In the li - ons' den he still be - lieved in God; so when tro - uble comes, let's learn to trust in God! D'you

Copyright © Gareth and Steve Hutchinson 2012

Chorus
21
C D G C Am7
wanna trust God like Da-niel did? The trust he had, it made him live God's way,
26
G/B
1.2.
D
To Intro
3.
D
Bridge
G F
d'you wan-na live God's way?
way?
D'you wan-na live God's way, God's way,
32
G F G F
d'you wan-na live God's way, God's way, d'you wan-na live God's way, God's way,
36
1.
G F
To Chorus (D. 𝄋.)
2.
G
d'you wan-na live God's way, God's way?
D'you
God's way, God's way?

Learn and remember song — Trust in the Lord

Vicki Warwick
arr. Rachel and Dan Warwick

Intro ♩ = 94

1. Trust in the Lord with all your heart, nev-er re-ly on what you think you know, re-mem-ber the Lord in all you do, and He will show you the right way.

2. You will be wise in all you do if you do what this verse says, re-mem-ber this verse and where it's from, Pro-verbs three verse five and six.

© Scripture Union 2006

PHOTOCOPIABLE PAGE

THE ENGINE ROOM

Construction/craft templates

Voyage 1
Fruity veggie magnets

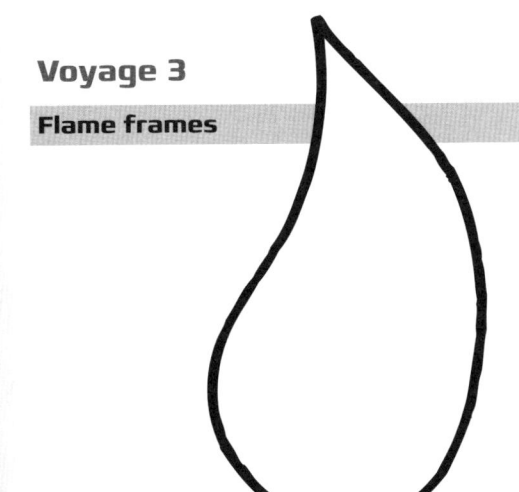

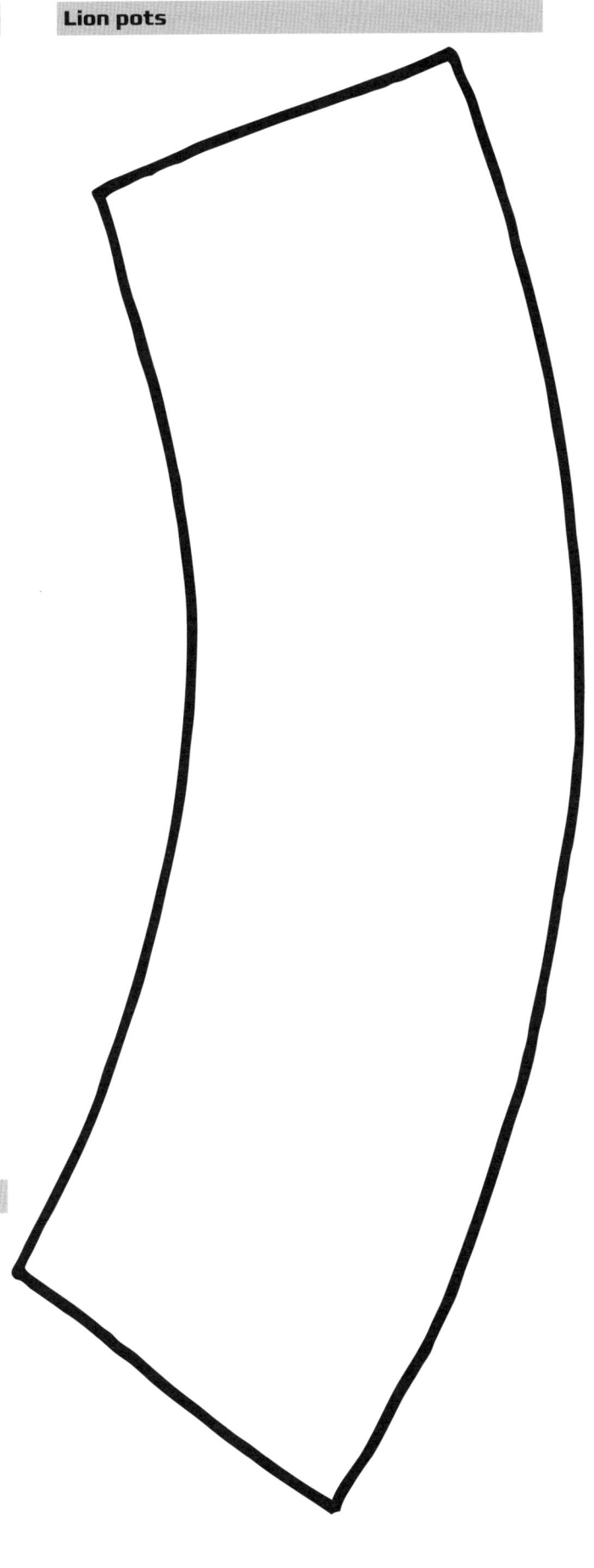

Apple

Carrot

Pineapple

Voyage 5
Lion pots

Voyage 3
Flame frames

CAPTAIN'S LOG 5

Game templates

Asteroids

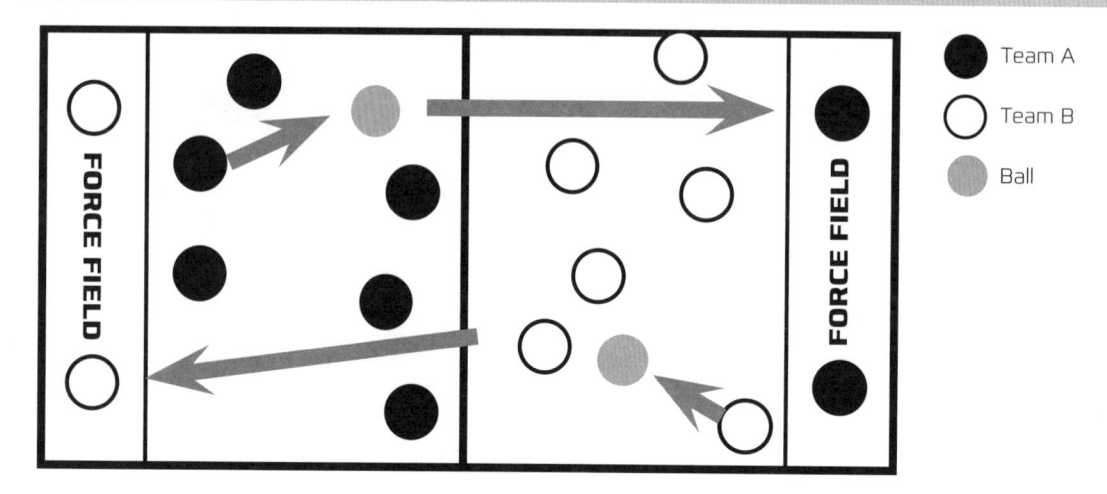

- Team A
- Team B
- Ball

FORCE FIELD

FORCE FIELD

Space Invaders

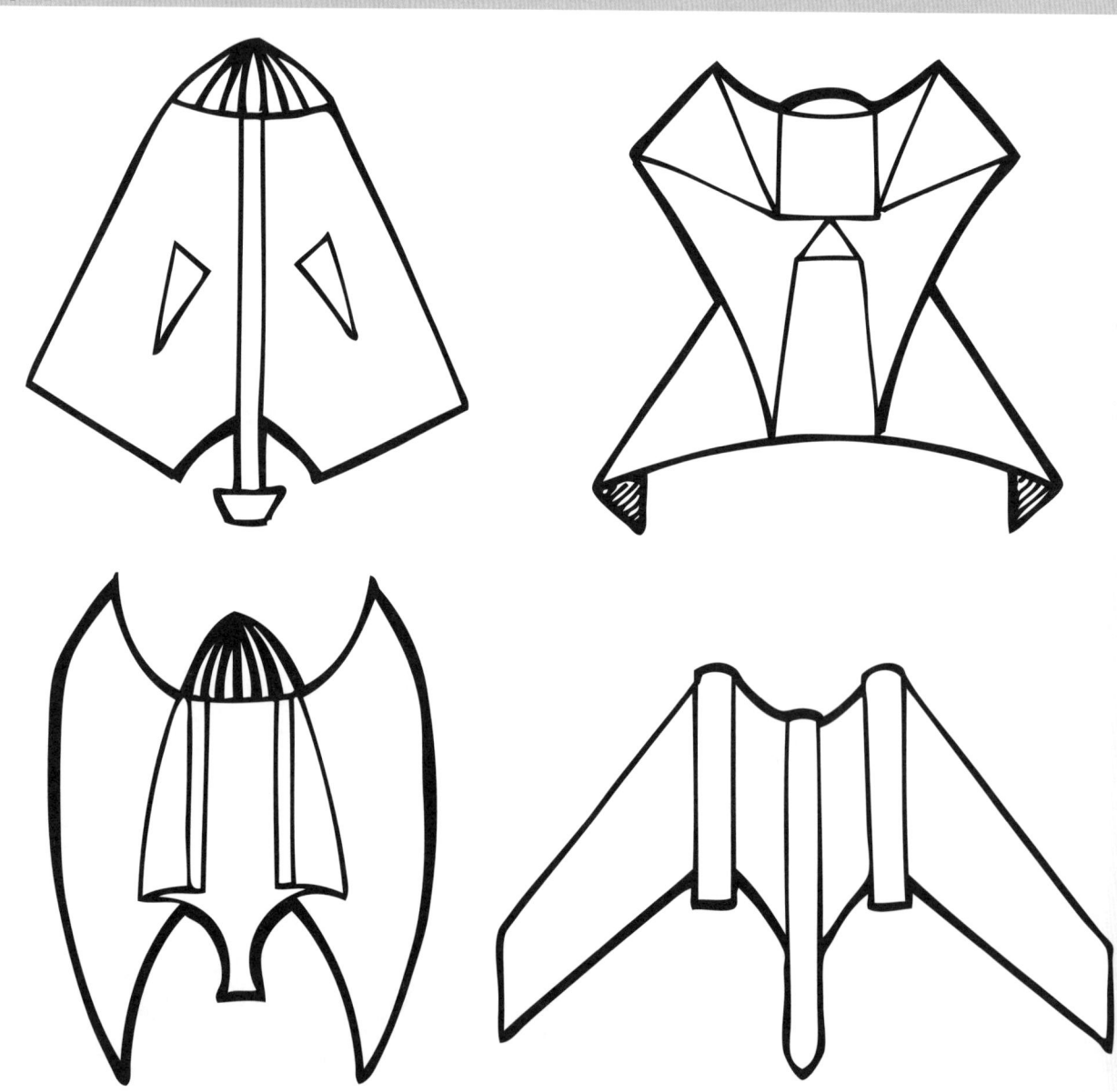

PHOTOCOPIABLE PAGE

THE ENGINE ROOM

Astronaut drive

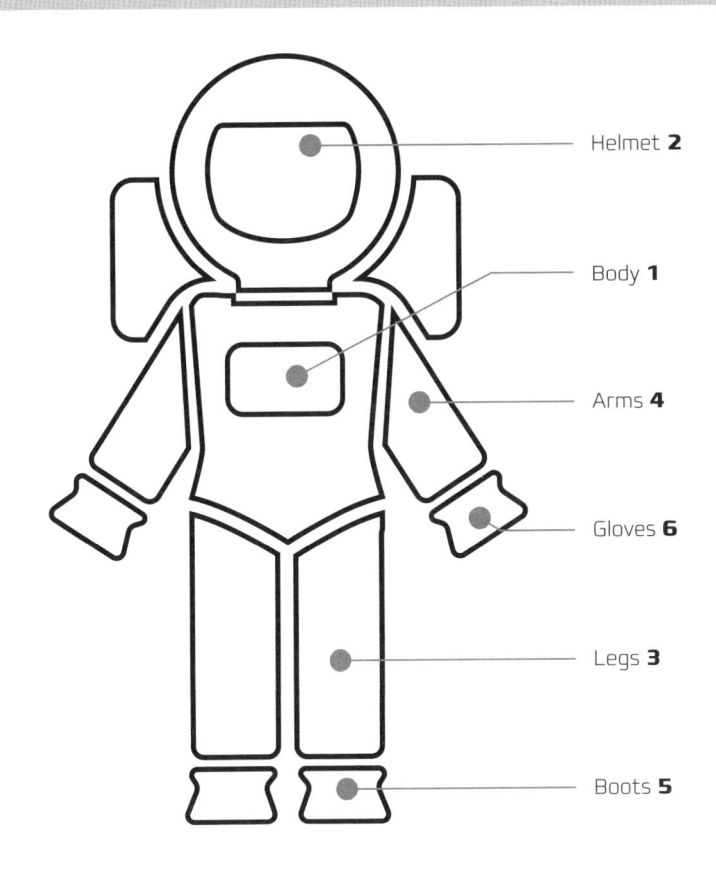

- Helmet **2**
- Body **1**
- Arms **4**
- Gloves **6**
- Legs **3**
- Boots **5**

Space code

a	b	c	d	e	f	g	h	i	j	k	l	m

n	o	p	q	r	s	t	u	v	w	x	y	z

CAPTAIN'S LOG **5**

91

CAPTAIN'S LOG 6

Following up **Space Academy**

Voyage beyond

Follow-up ideas

During your holiday club week you will more than likely make contact with children and families who have little or no regular contact with church. At *Space Academy* the children will have heard truths from the Bible, built positive relationships with your team and enjoyed being in community. It's a long time to wait until you do it all again next year! The following ideas aim to enable you to continue the important work you have begun and begin to disciple the children on a more regular basis, turning your holiday club ministry into a year-round ministry to children who may be currently outside the reach of your church.

Family ministry

It is vital to remember that children are part of families (however they might look) and that mission to the whole family is an essential part of passing on the stories and love of Jesus.

With a view to reaching the whole family, start inviting them to belong to the community, through events and in developing relationships. Once good relationships have been established, personal faith might be shared. This might take a long time to develop, but long-term commitment to children and families is essential. The ideas outlined below and those at www.exploretogether.org will provide you with some starting points for continuing the work with the children and for connecting with whole families.

Top Tips on Growing faith with families (SU, 978 1 84427 249 5, £2.99) is full of helpful advice if you're looking to start a family ministry.

Afternoon/evening activities

The *Space Academy* daily outlines provide enough material for one session: morning or afternoon. However, depending on the energy levels of your team and financial resources of your children/families/church, the holiday club lends itself to an optional extended programme, which could involve having a *Space Academy* room or event full of interesting facts and figures, images or videos about the universe and space travel. You could show the clip from the Apollo 11 moon landing or a clip from Apollo 13 where astronaut Jim Lovell (Tom Hanks) hosts a party for other astronauts and their families, and they watch on television as their colleague Neil Armstrong takes his first steps on the moon.

Include different ways for people to interact with the material you provide – eg, have some real astronaut food for them to rehydrate and taste. You could run games and/or craft afternoons using some of the more popular choices in *Space Academy*, together with options you didn't have time to try out during the club. You could even have some kind of sports competition! Events like these can be used to extend the *Space Academy* theme over the whole summer holidays if that's when you are running your club, with afternoon or evening events taking place in the weeks following the club.

One other idea to enhance the contact/maintain the relationship with the children who attend is to have a sleepover. You could do this (maybe with some fresh team!) on the last night of the club, perhaps after a family BBQ or, if you prefer, some months later when you could roll a Saturday night sleepover into a morning service and so invite and include those who were part of the holiday club but are not regular church attendees.

Family reunion evening

A family reunion event, which could be held in a half-term following *Space Academy*, allows children to revisit the ideas and themes of the club and to show their families the kinds of things they were involved in. Try to have as many of the *Space Academy* team available as possible, as this will help the children maintain the relationships they had at the club. Here is a suggested programme:

Report to Starbase

As the children arrive, they should go to their Starbases to catch up with each other. Play a game where you throw a dice and then talk about a specific topic assigned to the number you throw. Topics could include 'What I remember about *Space Academy*', 'What I did for the rest of my holidays' or 'What I like best about school'.

Meanwhile, parents could either join in with the groups or have a drink in a cafe area, where photographs and pieces of artwork from the week are displayed. Make this environment as warm and welcoming as possible and ensure that a number of team members are available to talk to parents and welcome them as they arrive.

Action stations

Sing the *Space Academy* song and play one of the mega games from the club. Explain the stories and themes of each day in the club. You could retell the most popular story from the week too.

Fit for space

Play some of the most popular games from *Space Academy*; you could even encourage the parents to take part!

Song and prayer

Choose a favourite song from the week to sing together, and then end with a prayer. Thank the parents for sending their children to the club and provide information about other up-and-coming events to be held at church.

Food

Share a simple meal together.

Midweek clubs

An ideal way to maintain contact with the children is to hold a midweek club at your church or local primary school. Scripture Union publishes *eye level* resources, aimed at midweek clubs for primary age children, especially those with no church background. Go to www.scriptureunion.org.uk/2368.id and choose any *eye level* club as a follow-up to *Space Academy*.

So Why God?, another *eye level* club, is suitable if you have children who are interested in knowing more about being a Christian. It takes questions children ask about following Jesus and helps them to come up with an answer. It also leads children in a sensitive way through the process of becoming a Christian. (See the inside front cover for details of *So Why God?*)

After-school activities

Many schools run after-school activities. A weekly *Space Academy* club could become a fantastic follow-up to the holiday club, engaging with the children where they are already at – in school. In negotiation with the head teacher and key members of staff, the club would be able to provide creative art workshops for children, including the telling of a Bible story and some opportunity for discussion. This would work best in small groups of no more than 12 children.

Space Academy days

Day events held throughout the year are good to maintain contact with holiday club children. These are effective when they coincide with a special time of the year: harvest, alternative Halloween, Christmas, new year, Valentine's Day, Easter. Here is a suggested programme:

- **Registration** and **Starbase games**
- **Action stations** (with story, teaching, songs, games, etc)
- **Games**
- **Break**
- **Small-group Bible exploration**
- **Lunch**
- **Craft**
- **Break**
- **Red alert!** (songs, Learn and remember verse, recap on story, interview)
- **Starbase** time for interactive prayer and response time

It might also be possible to run additional *Space Academy* days when the local school has an inset day. Gathering a team may be more difficult as many will be at work, but it can be of real service to the community and to parents who need to be at work themselves.

Family days

The programme above need not be limited to children. There is something spiritual about families sharing and learning together. Ability is not necessary, and the children will enjoy helping adults in activities with which they are comfortable. Therefore, one option is to hold a *Space Academy* day to which you invite the family members of the children who attended the holiday club. (Parents, siblings, grandparents, aunts/uncles, godparents are all welcome!)

X:site

X:site is a children's event for 7- to 11-year-olds. Each event takes place every two months in towns, cities or whole areas and combines silly games, live music, videos, creative prayer, craft, drama, Bible stories and lots more so that everyone can learn about Jesus and have fun at the same time!

X:site is a great way to encourage children in your church by bringing them together with other children in their community – they will have such a good time that they will want to invite their friends to come too. **X:site** is organised in each area by a partnership of local churches; Scripture Union is really keen to see more **X:site** events happening around the country. With your help there could be one near you.

Check out our website and if you want to get involved get in touch with us. We would really love to hear from you!

£5* OFF!

Buy £60 worth of extra Space Academy resources and get £5 off!

Complete the name and address, tick the right boxes and cut out the voucher. Then:

- Take it to your local Christian bookshop.
- Send it to:

   Scripture Union Mail Order
   PO Box 5148
   Milton Keynes MLO
   MK2 2YX

   with your order and payment.

- Visit our online shop at **www.scriptureunion.org.uk** and place your order online, where the £5 discount will be applied.

* Applies only to **Space Academy** resource book, **Space Academy** DVD and **Daniel's Data** (singles and packs).

SPACE ACADEMY

Title

Name

Address

Postcode

Email

We would like to keep in touch with you by placing you on our mailing list. Would you prefer to be contacted by:

☐ post   ☐ email

☐ If you prefer not to be contacted, then please tick this box.

Scripture Union does not sell or lease its lists.

SPACE ACADEMY

This voucher cannot be exchanged for cash or any other merchandise, and cannot be used with any other offer. This offer includes the **Space Academy** resource book, **Space Academy** DVD and **Daniel's Data** (singles and packs). It does not include CPO merchandise. Only orders of £60 and above qualify for this offer.

To the retailer: Please accept this voucher as a discount payment.

Credit due: £5.00 less normal trade discount.
This voucher must be returned by **4 September 2013** to:

Marston Book Services Ltd
PO Box 269
Abingdon
Oxfordshire
OX14 4YN

Shop name

Marston account no

Cash value: 0.0001p

VOSA13